MISTRESS OF CHARLECOTE

MISTRESS OF CHARLECOTE

The Memoirs of Mary Elizabeth Lucy

Introduced by
ALICE FAIRFAX-LUCY

LONDON
VICTOR GOLLANCZ LTD
1983

Published in association with Tigerlily Ltd

British Library Cataloguing in Publication Data
Lucy, Mary Elizabeth
   Mistress of Charlecote.
   1. Lucy, Mary Elizabeth
   I. Title   II. Fairfax-Lucy, Alice
   941.081'092'4   DA536.L/

   ISBN 0-575-03286-3

Photoset in Great Britain by
Rowland Phototypesetting Ltd, Bury St Edmunds, Suffolk
and printed by St Edmundsbury Press
Bury St Edmunds, Suffolk

Contents

Illustrations

House party at Four Oaks with Sir William Hartop, his family, and members of the Lucy family

Introduction

In the early dusk of a December day in the year 1823, a bride of twenty came to her husband's house in Warwickshire, driving down an avenue lined with cheering villagers brandishing torches; it was a fairy-tale welcome for a young girl who had never left her home for any but the briefest visits.

Charlecote Old Hall had been built in the first year of the reign of the first Elizabeth, who honoured it by a two-day visit. Set in water meadows of the Warwickshire Avon, it was an impressive gable-ended house with turrets at its four corners; the family of Lucy had lived on that piece of land since the twelfth century and in the course of six hundred years had acquired property that stretched across the whole county. They had been unwitting hosts to genius when the son of a tanner four miles down the river was caught stealing a buck in Charlecote Park. Since Sir Thomas Lucy was a Justice of the Peace, young William Shakespeare thought it prudent to remove himself to London, there to find employment in the theatre. This legend hallowed Charlecote.

The pattern of life in the deep country had changed very little since the repressive years of the Commonwealth and the restoration of the monarchy in 1660. Country gentlemen of moderate means and conservative tastes lived in their ancient halls and manor-houses in comparative comfort, though hearths smoked, window panes rattled and powerful draughts lifted carpets off the worn stone flags. This was the state of Charlecote when in the first quarter of the nineteenth century its owner, George Lucy, brought home his bride, Miss Mary Elizabeth Williams, an heiress from North Wales.

Lucys had married heiresses before, and sired large families, but over the last two centuries the place had not gone in direct descent from father to son and uncertainty fostered neglect: some of the rooms were perpetually shuttered and weeds grew in the court. George Lucy had begun to remedy things and by 1823 the home farms sent up plentiful beef and cream, apricots and peaches flourished in the huge kitchen garden, there was venison from the descendants of Shakespeare's deer. The Elizabethan house was surrounded by a park of dream-like beauty, through which the river Avon took its stately course, and from whose timber George Lucy had paid his father's debts.

Mary Elizabeth Lucy was to have many children and, in her eighties, while her rheumatic hands could still wield a quill, she decided to set down for her posterity the story of her life, recapturing a cloudlessly happy childhood, a first love affair, her wedding and the arrival by torchlight at the house that was to be her home. Writing of the early years her pen races like a catspaw of wind crisping a sunny pond. She never loses sight of the girl she once was; a contemporary of Jane Austen's heroines, tiny and quick in her movements with piled-up black curls on a little head set on a long neck, blushing at compliments (in middle age the high colour was to become fixed in her cheeks).

The pages that follow are the record of a happy life written down in five black notebooks with marbled end-papers bought from a stationer in Warwick. Not a life without its anguish and regrets—for the husband who died, the lovely children who faded like flowers—but an existence founded on the calm certainties of the Age of Progress. She lived through the high noon of the Victorian squirearchy, foreseeing golden years succeeding golden years toward a harvest that would scatter even richer blessings on England and her Empire. But Mary Elizabeth's recollections are not of politics and world affairs, they cover a narrow range (except for a tour in Europe in the 1840s); her children and grandchildren, her garden, her loved parents, her dear brothers, the church, the village, are enough to fill her life. There are visits, some enjoyable, some not; there is her proficiency on the harp; family marriages, dramas and deaths; always coming back to Charlecote, 'that dear old place where sorrow and happiness have been so intertwined . . .' coming at last to the 'dear snug little room' that was to be her refuge in old age.

Today its coved ceiling is spoiling with damp and time, some of the gilt scrolls from the tall mirror over the marble mantel, which reflects only sky and the tops of the trees, have broken off; a rich fur of dust is on everything. On red velvet, modelled in plaster, are a baby's hand curled up in an adult's and her own hand with the harpist's spatulate thumb and first finger holding a pen. Like Queen Victoria, whose sitting room at Osborne this room closely resembles, she crowded every inch of space with children's likenesses; every object of ruby glass, white Parian ware, variegated marble, buhl and tortoiseshell (still lying where she left them) had tender associations for her, marking the emotional milestones of her eighty-seven years.

The coming of dusk, the tucking of cushions in her back, the wheeling forward of the davenport that held her letters and diaries were the preliminaries to a congenial ramble through her memories.

It would be very quiet in this room which is so high above the river; the only sounds to invade the stillness would be the grumble of the scullery pump a long way down below, the cascade's continuous whisper, audible only in the pauses of the wind, and from across the river the sound of the stags roaring through the autumn mist.

THE MEMOIRS OF
MARY ELIZABETH LUCY

The Sunshiny Morning of Youth

It is bitter cold and as I am only just recovering from an attack
of bronchitis I dare not venture to leave my own dear, warm,
snug little room, and am too weak to play on my harp and am
tired of reading, so I have much leisure, and fancy it will amuse
me to write, and perhaps one day it will amuse my dear
grandchildren to read, my reminiscences of when I was
young.

I was born on the 25th of November 1803 at the beautiful
and dearly loved family seat, Boddlewyddan in the county of
Flint in North Wales. My parents were Sir John Williams,
Bart., and Margaret his wife, who was a Miss Williams of
Trefry in Anglesea and a Welsh heiress. I had two brothers,
John and Hugh, and three sisters, Harriet, Emma and Mar-
garet, older than myself, and one brother, William, and one
sister Ellin, younger.

I can just remember my maternal grandmother who lived
with us. I loved her dearly, she taught me my letters, and to
spell cat and dog, and to read that nice old-fashioned book
Cobwebs to Catch Flies. She died quite soon after Ellin was
born. I was in such trouble at her death that the only way to
dry my tears was to give me the baby to nurse. I used to fancy
she was my very own child. I was always devoted to dolls, but
whenever I was allowed to have the little Ellin my doll was put
away.

15

As we three younger ones grew in stature we grew to love each other and were inseparable—the five elder ones seemed quite distinct from us. We slept in cribs in the nursery, which was a very large room with two tall windows. Nurse had an old-fashioned four-post bed and in the early morning when she got up it was our delight to get into it, draw the curtains and have a game of romps, knocking each other down with the pillows. Nurse was one of the race of tale-telling nurses, and whenever we were naughty she used to say a witch would come and take us off through the window. There was a most horrid old woman named Grassy, with a fearful front tooth like an elephant's tusk, who used to come and help in the wash house, and her husband, a frightful man called Long Peter (for he was quite a giant) who used to brew. And with these two dreadful people Nurse used to terrify us by threatening to call them in and bid them carry us off.

After Grand Mamma's death, my own darling Mamma taught me everything, and heard me say my prayers. She bid me love God and try to be good and obedient and then God would love me and watch over me.

These extra happy childish days began to change when Willy was old enough to go to school. I was to have a governess, my elder sisters having done with the schoolroom; Sister (as Harriet was called, being the eldest) went to Bath to stay with an old maiden aunt, Papa's sister, and have masters, and Emma and Margaret (who we called Miggy) went to an uncle, Fleetwood Williams, Papa's youngest brother who lived in London, to have music and dancing masters.

My governess's name was Blackburn, she was very handsome and very good, but so strict. Oh! so strict! She used at first to frighten my wits away. I began lessons at six o'clock in summer and seven in winter, and had to forfeit a penny for every five minutes I was behind time. Breakfast was at eight, a bowl of bread and milk and nothing else until I entered my teens. And from that day I have never so much as tasted bread and milk. There was a closet in the schoolroom where we kept our exercise books and where Miss Blackburn had a loaf of bread, a slice of which she used to eat for her luncheon. Whenever I was turned with [stuck in] my lesson or showed the least sign of rebellion and temper or impatience, she would shut me up in this closet, which I dreaded above everything as I was so afraid of the mice that used to come after her bread, and were legion. And there I had to remain till I could say with a cheerful voice that I was quite good. She was really *over*-strict for if I only missed a word in repeating perhaps a page of history or a long piece of poetry she would often double the punishment. Ellin was in the schoolroom with me and, poor little soul, was forever in the closet.

We had a half-holiday on Saturdays and a whole one on our birthdays, and though we never had children's parties, on these occasions we were always very happy and merry, and dined with Papa and Mamma. Nurse, dressed in her silk gown, lace ruff and cap with a large bow of blue riband, used to come in at dessert to give her blessing and drink the health of the one whose natal day we were celebrating.

On the 9th of January, John, my eldest brother's birthday, there was always a dance to which all the neighbours were invited and it was delightful. I was so fond of dancing (and so proud I recall of a new white muslin frock and white satin sash) that I never went to bed till the end when Sir Roger de Coverly was danced.

Our chief neighbours were the Hughes of Kinmel, the Heskeths of Gwrgch Castle, the Lloyds of Penwern, the Pennants of Downing, the Mostyns of Telacre, Mrs Browne of Bronwylfa with her two daughters Harriett (the most talented musician) and Felicia, Mrs Hemans the gifted poetess. The celebrated Mrs Piozzi of Brynbella was not far away and often spent a few days with us. She was a very pretty little old lady always dressed in black satin with a black satin hat turned up over a wig of brown curls, and to my inexperienced eye a beautiful complexion, but, alas, like Jezebel she painted her face! I wondered why her cheeks were such a lovely pink, when one evening when she was gone downstairs to dinner her maid met me in the passage and said 'Miss Mary, would you like to come and help me tidy my Mistress's room?'

The first thing that attracted my notice was a hare's foot on her toilette table, and taking it up I exclaimed, 'What can this be for?'

'Well,' she replied, opening a small box of rouge, 'it is to put this rouge on her face with.'

I begged the maid to put some on my cheeks but she would not, and told me I must not say a word to anyone about the hare's foot and the rouge.

Mrs Piozzi's first husband was Mr Thrale of Streatham, and during his lifetime Dr Johnson (who wrote the Dictionary) was her dearest and most devoted friend and quite made his home with them. He used to liken her to a fluttering butterfly.

Signor Piozzi was an Italian singing-master and a very fascinating man. She accidentally made his acquaintance in 1780 and was at once attracted to him, and asked him to give lessons to her daughters. From that time he became quite intimate with the Thrales, staying constantly at Streatham and for three years he taught the Miss Thrales their do, re, mi, fa. Then Mr Thrale died and very soon after she wrote to Dr Johnson to announce her intended marriage with Signor Piozzi. His reply to this extraordinary news was an angry, even contemptuous appeal to her, imploring her not to make a laughing stock of herself. She was furious and renounced his friendship, virtually bidding him attend to his own concerns.

Mary Elizabeth was to have her very first music lesson with Signor Piozzi, picking out the notes while sitting on his knee at the parlour organ in the upstairs sitting room of Brynbella which lies across the valley of the Clwyd from Boddlewyddan.

As I grew older I became daily fonder of study, I was passionately fond of music and drawing. We had an organ in the hall and Papa made me play Handel to him every Sunday evening. He was a fine performer himself on the violoncello. I longed to learn the harp but Miggy had chosen that, to me, most lovely instrument, so I was not allowed to learn it.

Nurse told me one day that Kitty, the housemaid, and John, the schoolroom boy, who waited on us and cleaned our shoes, were both so anxious to be able to read and write, so I undertook to teach them whenever I could in my play hours. They came with me to an upstairs landing where no one would interrupt us, and I brought my spelling book and slate and did my best. But they were so stupid, it required the patience of Job to get them to remember the alphabet. However, 'there is as much wisdom in the desire of being instructed as there is in the knowledge itself'. There were no village schools in the days of my youth in our part of the world so the peasants grew up quite uneducated. But alas, I must say, with all the over schooling of the present day the race of old faithful servants is fast dying away.

From my earliest childhood I was taught never to touch or meddle with anything that was not my own. Dearest Mamma once took me with her to visit two old ladies, Lady Eleanor Butler and Miss Sara Ponsonby, who lived together in a beautiful cottage at Llangollen and had no end of pretty things in their drawing room. I looked and admired everything and thought how much I should like to have some of them in my hand but I remembered what I had been taught. When we were going away the old ladies said, 'Come, dear little Mary, and give us a kiss for you have been so good and not meddled with any of our pretty things, so we shall be glad to see you here again and here's a nice peach for you.' (The little thatched summer house in Charlecote's garden by the orangery I copied from what I remembered of that visit and furnished it with child-sized tables and chairs to amuse my children and their children after them.) These two ladies looked just like two old men. They always dressed in dark cloth habits with short skirts, high shirt collars, white cravats and men's hats, with their hair cut short. When they walked out (they never rode on horseback) they carried a stick to look like a whip and an Italian greyhound was their constant companion. They were so devoted to each other that they made a vow, and kept it, that they would never marry or be separated, but would always live together in their cottage and never leave it or sleep out for even one night.

I idolised my mother, she was the most perfect character, not to be bettered and hardly to be equalled. She was always instilling good into us, and when she had occasion to reprove us she did it in so sweet and gentle a manner that you could not help (at least I could not) putting your arms round her neck and kissing her with your eyes full of tears and your heart full of repentance. She had us every morning to read the psalms, and in the evening Ellin and I read the evening psalms with Miss Blackburn. Miss Blackburn was a thoroughly religious woman and very clever, her information without being profound was general. She was a good linguist, I learnt French and Italian with her, German was not then the fashion as it is now. She was very particular in making me do plain sewing and I was very proud when I made Willy a shirt all by myself and had a whole shilling as a reward. I used to make baby clothes and flannel petticoats for the village women. Miss Blackburn was most charitable and encouraged me to give at least a third of my little pocket money to the poor, instead of spending it on trifles for myself. She was a strict observer of Lent, and as far as I could I tried to follow her example and deny myself whatever I liked best.

Brother (John), who was at a private tutor's, was so good-natured and when he came home for Easter he used to take me on some pleasant expedition; my greatest pleasure was to take my basket and go with him to gather wild roses in a wood called Penny Gurig about half a mile away. We were never allowed to go there alone as there were many old mine shafts, for there used to be lead found there. I never saw anywhere such beautiful briar roses, not only white and pink but the deepest rose colour, almost crimson, and such a variety of wild flowers; such joy for me when I found a bee orchis. Then sometimes I would go with him to fish in the Clwyd, he caught delicious small trout but I had only a poor worm and got hardly a bite. When I was tired of this I would sit on a stone and get him to tell me stories out of the Arabian Nights.

One Christmas Brother's tutor, Mr Jones, came to stay at Boddlewyddan. We had great fun with him for he was so absent minded. One morning at breakfast he asked if he might boil an egg for himself as he was very particular as to its being done for exactly three minutes. So a saucepan was brought and he took out his watch, looked at the time, then put the watch in the saucepan and took the egg and held it in his hand. When he thought the three minutes were expired he found to his horror that he had boiled the watch instead of the egg. Everyone burst out laughing and the poor man, looking at Brother, said, 'John, why did you not tell me what I was doing? For Lord bless my soul! I have spoilt my watch.'

When I was about twelve years old I met with a sad accident by falling out of a swing. The ropes were attached to two high trees and you had to sit in the centre of them. My brothers and elder sisters had all been swung and it was my turn. A gardener who happened to be passing stopped and said, 'Shall I give you a good swing, Miss Mary?'

'Oh, do!'

'Well, hold tight then,' and I held as tight as I could but he gave the swing such a push that he jerked me off and down I fell on my face. My nose was nearly smashed and my mouth cut in all directions. My teeth were loosened but happily not broken. When I got up, covered with blood, they were so frightened and Brother carried me to a little brook close by and washed my face and vainly tried to wash my frock, but finding the blood was flowing faster and faster from my nose and mouth, they took me home. Nurse immediately got a great slice of raw beef and covered my face with it. Dr Davis was sent for and he ordered me to lie quiet and still in bed and be patient, and there he left me for three long weeks. Nurse fed me with a quill for I could not open my mouth wide enough to eat anything, which was miserable.

When I was well enough, Mamma took me to a dentist in Liverpool who had a reputation for being very clever, but I did not think him clever at all for he proposed taking all my teeth out, setting them in gold, and then putting them back into my mouth. He said my lower jaw was broken and consequently my teeth must in time drop out, they could never be firm again. But I declared he should not touch them and begged and prayed so hard that Mamma yielded to my entreaties; and how fortunate for me! For here I am, 80 years of age with all my teeth still sound, though I suffered for many a long day.

Now, my dear grandchildren, when you read what I am about to write don't laugh and say 'Granny must be very vain to have remembered what was said of her so long ago!' But no. I never was vain of my beauty. I knew it was God's gift and from no merit of my own, and with youth it would fade.

Once, when I had been unwell and was lying on the sofa in the schoolroom, I, heard the door open and Dora Allanson with Emma and Miggy came in. I did not want to be disturbed so shut my eyes and pretended to be fast asleep. Dora said, 'Hush, don't wake her,' and then on tip-toe came close to me and after standing some minutes by the sofa I heard her say to the others, 'How lovely she is. She will eclipse you all when she comes out.' After they had gone out of the room, I got up and looked at myself in a looking-glass and thought, 'Am I really so lovely?' I thought Miggy much prettier.

It was the fashion for girls to wear caps in the morning when you were in your teens. I was the family milliner for I often made caps for dear Mamma (I find in an old pocket book that Mamma gave me 2d for making her a black cap, and for making her six night-caps, 9d). The Pennants were coming to stay. I had made a cap for myself like a baby's of simple blonde net with a ruche of tulle round it, and I pinned a pink rose out of my garden on one side of it. Miggy was wild when she saw it, she was so in love with David Pennant (I think he was the handsomest man I ever saw) and thought he would admire her in a cap like mine. I was very fond of him, too. There is a Welsh superstition that if you find a twig on an ash tree with two leaves at the top instead of one as they mostly grow, you are sure to marry the man whose Christian name is the same as the man's you first meet when you have such a twig in your hand. Miggy and I, who fully believed it, would run off to the garden hoping to meet the under-gardener whose name was David; but alas, our handsome David married before I even came out.

I was now about 16 and caused Papa at last to let me learn the harp, and many a shilling he gave me when I played to please him. I had lessons too in singing. Miggy had a lovely soprano voice and mine being contralto we sang duets.

In 1820, Brother's birthday falling on a Sunday, we had our annual Ball on the 10th and it was a charming one, a real Ball, all the County were at it. Dancing began at nine o'clock and continued till four in the morning. I danced every dance and had David Pennant several times for my partner. The waltz was not yet known outside London Society; we danced only country dances, quadrilles and reels. At the time of the Ball, Mr B. O., a friend of Brother's stayed a week at Boddlewy-ddan. My sisters, one and all, thought him perfect, so good looking, so tall and with such an elegant figure. Miggy compared him to the Duke of Devonshire. His *greatest* charm was that he had ten thousand a year, a fine place, and a splendid collection of pictures. (Emma, my second sister, painted wonderfully well in oils and he said he should take great pleasure in lending her some of his pictures to copy, and was as good as his word, for on his return home he sent her one by Mieris, the subject was the interior of a shop, a work of the highest excellence and she made an admirable copy of it.)

Mr B. O. came again and stayed till the 5th of June. Emma made sure she should be Mrs B. O. and Miggy flattered herself *she* should, and it was such fun, Brother joining in and teasing them both. I rejoiced when he went away for he bored me so and was forever after me in my garden, begging cuttings from different plants. Miss Price, my new governess, arrived on the very day he left. She was very clever and I soon made great progress for she had such an admirable and pleasant way of imparting knowledge. I read with her all the best works in French—Racine, Corneille, Molière—and in Italian Tasso and Petrarch—and for the first time Shakespeare and Sir Walter Scott. How I did delight in them!

In the autumn, a friend of Brother's, John Lucy, Rector of Hampton Lucy in Warwickshire, but quite a young man, came to stay and accompanied us to Holywell Races. I had never been on a race-course or seen a race and was wild with the excitement of it. The Reverend Lucy amused us with a story of Sir Edward Mostyn of Telacre (a fine place near Holywell) with whom he had been staying. Sir Edward and his wife (they were Roman Catholics) had been separated for many years but were on friendly terms. He was particularly fond of sport and invited a number of gentlemen, including Mr Lucy, to shoot partridges with him; but on the first morning at breakfast he sent for Mr Lucy to come to his private room, and holding out a letter with a deep black border, said, 'See this, Lucy, I have just received it announcing the death of Lady Mostyn. Here, take it, re-seal it, put it in your pocket and let me have it tomorrow. Mind you don't say a word about it for I know my poor dear wife, good soul, would say if she could, "don't let my death spoil your day's sport, but go and enjoy it with your friends".' So he did, and they had a capital day, killing I don't know how many birds. The next morning he had the black-edged letter, his friends were told the sad contents and all took their leave.

Shortly afterwards, Papa, Mamma, Sister, Emma and Mr B. O. (who for the third time had turned up) went to Wynnstay for the christening of the son and heir of Sir Watkyn Williams-Wynne. Brother and Mr John Lucy went to stay with friends at Erthig for it. The baby was so large, weighing 13 pounds the day he was born, that when he was shown to the tenants one old Welsh farmer called out 'He is just the weight of a Welsh goose!' There was a Ball after the christening. Our party all returned the following day. Emma was in the greatest state of excitement and when they got home rushed after Papa and said she wanted to speak to him. He took her into his own room and asked her what she had to say. She answered that Mr B. O. had proposed to her last night at the Wynnstay Ball. Papa was pleased. He sent for Mr B. O. and told him what Emma had said and how happy he should be to have him for a son-in-law. Mr B. O. was thunder-struck and declared he had never made her an offer; if he had said anything of the kind he must have had too much champagne, but he added, 'My dear Sir John, I still hope I may be your son-in-law if you will give me Mary, your fourth daughter, to be my wife', etc., and left the room. Papa then had poor Emma back and told her she must be mistaken, for the young man declared he had never made her any such offer. She persisted he had and bursting into a flood of tears sobbed out 'Well, at any rate he did *all but*!'

Papa did not say a word about me. Mr B. O. then made a formal proposal for my hand. My parents said he had their consent if he had mine, only he must wait till I was older. Then Mamma called me into her sitting room and told me what had happened and that he was waiting to speak to me. I screamed out 'No, no, I won't see him. Oh, do persuade him to marry Emma! I don't love him one bit—Emma does.' And I flew back to the schoolroom. I would never marry him nor would I see him again, so he left Boddlewyddan in a state of despair. I begged Papa and Mamma not to tell anyone and they promised they would not. But Brother knew everything and from that time used to call poor Emma All But, and even made up a play about it.

My seventeenth birthday falling in the December of that year (1820), I was now a come-out young lady but by my own wish I continued in the schoolroom. I have lost my pocket book for the following year so cannot refresh my memory with anything in particular that occurred except that Brother went abroad and visited Florence, Rome, etc., and at Lyons bought an exquisite dress which he intended to give to whichever sister married first. Also I became so fond of drawing that year and spent a great deal of time drawing and painting from nature on rice paper every butterfly that could be caught—and they were legion. I never see so many now, or such beauties.

It was on the morning of the 30th of September of the following year that we four sisters set off in the phaeton (the servants with our luggage following in a chaise) to stay with Miss Hesketh of Tulketh in Lancashire for the Preston Guild, which is held every 21 years and lasts a fortnight. It was the first time I had been visiting without my own dear Mamma and I did so long for her. The party staying at Tulketh (which is only a few miles from Preston) consisted of the Heskeths of Rossal (cousins of ours), their sons Peter and Charles, and a Mr Wilson Patten, the only son of Colonel Wilson Patten of Bank Hall—*such* a handsome young man.

On the Monday, the Mayor of Preston's Procession was held, every tradesman walking by twos in costume denoting their several callings, and in the evening a ball where I danced every dance, oftenest with the 'handsome young man'. We certainly were attracted to each other at first sight. The following days were crammed with entertainment: at the Mayor's reception, with everyone in full Court dress with plumes of ostrich feathers, the Countess of Derby (Miss Farren the actress) appeared with a bird of Paradise on her head and lovely humming birds on the body and sleeves of her dress (these had been given her by Mr Warburton, the greater traveller). Lord Derby called and sat some time and made himself very agreeable. I saw a balloon go up for the first time and thought it wonderful. There were oratorios (the Creation, the Messiah), balls every night, races and a masquerade.

On Monday the 16th we all went to Rossal and Mr Wilson Patten went with us. He left Rossal the day before us but we parted lovers, having exchanged hearts. We were not be-

26

trothed because he was not of age and so went home to ask his father's consent to our marriage which was refused. But the heart that has truly loved never forgets . . .

Soon after their return to Boddlewyddan Sir John called her into his study to hear Colonel Wilson Patten's letter saying that he was sending his son abroad to complete his studies and to forget Miss Mary Elizabeth, as it was hoped she would forget him. This she never did. He was to come back into her life much later and, after her husband's death, to propose marriage again.

The following year (1822) dear Miggy went to London for the Season with Lady Harriett Williams-Wynne. She came home having enjoyed herself immensely. She confided to me that she thought she had made a conquest of Mr George Lucy of Charlecote, the Rev. John's brother. She had met him a number of times in London and he had danced with her and promised to come to Boddlewyddan in the autumn as Brother had invited him. They had become acquainted at a private tutor's.

On the 20th of August he did come, bringing with him two lively cousins, Newton and Leveson Lane. I perfectly well remember Miggy and I standing on the balcony out of Mamma's room and seeing a carriage with four post horses drive up, and a smart valet jump off the box to ring the bell and open the carriage door. As three young men alighted she pointed out to me which was Mr Lucy and then flew downstairs to welcome him, as Brother happened to be out. That evening after dinner we had music—harp, piano and singing—and then danced quadrilles until bedtime, and this was repeated every evening (Sundays excepted) during the fortnight the three cousins stayed with us. Mr Lucy always asked me to dance much oftener than any of my sisters. I was so sorry for I knew it vexed Miggy and indeed it vexed myself for I preferred dancing with Newton or Leveson Lane who were much more lively and younger, only a few years older than I was.

I shall now skip over the next six weeks to when my fate was sealed. On the 14th of October 1823 Mr Lucy came again to Boddlewyddan and at the close of the week Papa sent for me and told me Mr Lucy had asked for my hand. In an agony I fell on my knees and implored him to refuse, as I did not, *could not* love him. I cried 'Oh why won't he have Miggy who does!'

However Papa would not listen to me and insisted on my submission, so my tears were in vain. I had been brought up to obey my parents in everything and, though I dearly loved Papa, I had always rather feared him. I felt I dared not disobey him so went into the library and there found Mr Lucy waiting to ask me to be his wife. I was so agitated that I never remembered what he said or what I said, all I knew was that he put a beautiful turquoise hoop on my finger and I rushed out of the room and flew upstairs to my own precious darling Mamma, telling her everything and weeping bitterly. She kissed and kissed me again and again, and said all she could to comfort me, adding 'My sweet Mary, love *will come* when you know all of Mr Lucy's good qualities'—and it did come—but oh the sunshiny morning of youth. . . .

The Lucys of Charlecote had descended in a long if not unbroken line, living and multiplying on the same piece of Warwickshire earth as had first been granted by the Conqueror to one of his Norman followers. De Charlecotes became de Lucys, fought at Crécy and Agincourt and rushed towards the rising sun of the Tudors. George Lucy's father, a clergyman from Cheshire, had succeeded a bachelor Lucy cousin. He sent his sons (John the younger was to become Rector of Hampton Lucy) to Eton and Winchester, Christ Church, Oxford, and Trinity, Cambridge, and, proud of George's intellectual attainments, bought for him a Pocket Borough so that he could write MP after his name. George Lucy was the sort of precise, cultivated young man who might have remained a bachelor pursuing intellectual interests all his life, had he not so much wished to prolong his line. If in the first place he had had thoughts of Mary Elizabeth's dowry (a lead mine was the

Lady Williams

Sir John Williams of Boddlewyddan

Mary Elizabeth Williams

Margaret 'Miggie' Williams

Boddlewyddan, the Williams family seat in North Wales

George Lucy of Charlecote, who married at 34

Mary Elizabeth Lucy, painted shortly after her marriage

Carry, Spencer, Fulke and Emily in 1832

Charlecote before restoration

Mary Elizabeth in her late thirties

Pastel drawing of MEL in Rome shows Herbie, who had died two years earlier

Charlecote after restoration; a new wing was also added on the left

'Brother'

Lady Willoughby de Broke

Herbert Almeric

William Fulke at Eton

Emily Fitzhugh

Mr Thomas

House party at Four Oaks with Sir William Hartop: MEL in the centre, Spencer left, and young Berkeley on the steps

source of the Williams' ample fortune), this thought was now at the
back of his mind, so enchanting did he find her. He was an old
thirty-four, she made him feel a boy again.

The news spread like wildfire, and congratulations poured in
from all parts, neighbours continually calling and I being sent
for to receive their good wishes, etc. but was hardly ever to be
found, for as soon as I heard the doorbell ring I flew into the
nursery (which was still the room where Ellin and I slept) and
made old Nurse lock the door. I felt so shy, I could not bear
being stared at as the bride elect, and I used to dread meeting
anyone on the daily rides and drives that Mr Lucy and I made
together.

On the 29th October Mr Lucy, with Brother, left Boddlewyddan on their way to Charlecote to prepare and make it
ready for its new mistress. I must here transcribe in part my
first love-letter (which, with many more, I still have).

'I cannot omit the first opportunity, my dearest Mary, of
writing a few lines. It seems an age since we parted and yet it
is but three days. I was up last night and the night before at
balls but they did not yield me the usual delight, nor
dissipate the *ennui* and restlessness I feel away from your
sweet company.

Do preserve the affectionate letters you speak of, to read
them will be such a pleasure, as well as to see the pretty
presents which must be regarded as so many marks of
friendship and affection, and are the best evidence of the
interest you excite and the estimation in which you are
held—really, I do not say too much when I say that you are
the delight of all circles and the Idol of your own. Indeed I
shall never cease to style myself the most fortunate and
happiest of mankind. You may imagine after the lapse of a
century how much is required to be done at Charlecote,
which in time I hope we shall accomplish. Your taste and
wishes I shall always consult but I am anxious to make the

house a little comfortable for your reception so have been very busy.'

He wrote to me nearly every day. He returned to Boddle-wyddan a month later and brought me the most magnificent presents for my twentieth birthday: an exquisite Brussels lace veil, splendid diamond earrings composed of several stones of the finest water, a complete set of rubies and diamonds set in massive gold, and diamond and ruby rings.

The wedding was to take place on December 2nd. Dear old Nurse was in despair at the thought of parting with me for I was her special pet. I used from childhood to sit and read the Bible to her whenever I was able, while she darned our stockings, her favourite and constant occupation. I always made her caps. 'Oh! My dear Miss Mary,' she lamented, 'what shall I do without you? Who will read God's holy word to me? Or make my caps?' I said, 'I will always be your milliner, dear Nurse and make you a lot before I am Mrs Lucy,' and I set to work at once and made her two dozen, and she was delighted.

And now the eventful Tuesday, the 2nd of December, was come, and though more than sixty years have passed since then every incident is fresh in my memory. I fancy I see that dear old Nurse with trembling hands and tears dimming her eyes, dressing me—her own dear child as she often used to call me—in my bridal robe of snow-white silk which she entreated she might do, and then standing by to watch my new lady's maid, Turner, arrange my hair and the wreath of orange blossoms, with the lace veil of texture fine as a spider's web falling over all. The bridesmaids, my four sisters, Charlotte Hughes of Kinmel, and Dora Allanson of Llanarch, were all dressed in simple white cashmere, their bonnets lined with pink, my favourite colour.

I can quite hear the clock strike three and the carriages are at the door. I get into the family coach drawn by Papa's own four beautiful black horses, followed by many more carriages, and

we arrive at St Asaph and find the Bishop of Luxmoor waiting
for us in the old Cathedral where no couple had in the memory
of man been joined together in the holy bands of matrimony
(we therefore had to be married by special licence). Then I
kneel at the altar beside him for whom I am 'to forsake all
others and keep only unto him so long as we both shall live'.

The solemnisation of matrimony over, as I rose from my
knees I fainted away. I was taken into the Bishop's pew, my
poor husband in an agony, looking at his bride and not
knowing what on earth to do, whilst darling Mamma and old
Nurse, weeping, chafed my hands and sprinkled water (hastily
fetched from the Palace) over my face. As soon as I was
recovered and all was attested in the vestry, Nurse wrapped
me in a large swan's down tippet which reached to my feet,
with my hands in a muff of swan's down large enough for a
harlequin to jump through (the fashion of the time). The
bridesmaids prepared to throw old satin shoes for good luck
and dearest Papa put me into my husband's new chariot
which, with four horses and postilions decked out with large
white favours, was waiting at the door of the cathedral to take
us 12 miles to Cerig Llwydion, my uncle Williams' seat, lent
us for our honeymoon.

How well I remember the first evening. After our *tête à tête*
dinner Mr Lucy did not leave the dining room with me and I
sat nearly a whole hour by myself in the dismal drawing
room, no piano even to amuse me, so I read my Bible and
Prayer Book, and then I thought of bye-past times, how calm,
how cloudless my childhood had passed, like a long long
happy summer holiday. And then again what sorrow filled my
heart when I thought of parting from my most dear parents
and the home that I so loved.

1824–1829

The Married Lady

The day after our marriage my husband asked me if I should like to go to London as this was such a dull place. I said, 'Oh, yes, for I have never been there.' So we left Cerig Llwydion on the 4th. As there were no railroads then it took us two days before our journey ended. We arrived in London late on the Saturday and went to Kirkham's Hotel in Brook Street. On Monday we drove half over London seeing sights till I was almost bewildered, but delighted. We went to Erard's and chose a harp (the very harp that my children and now my grandchildren play on) and went shopping, and my husband gave me endless beautiful and useful things—a writing desk and work box all so handsome in buhl, a fur cloak, silks, lovely lace, in fact anything I expressed the slightest wish for.

On December the 15th we left London and arrived at Charlecote the next evening, that now dearly-loved old place where past pleasures, pain, and sorrow have been so twined together. It was dusk when we drove through the Park gate and there was a torch-light procession of the tenantry drawn up by the old gateway to welcome us, and many were on the flat leaden roof with flambeaux in their hands to cheer and hurrah us as we passed underneath. The church bells were ringing forth their merry peals and the house blazed with lights from every window. The domestics all marshalled in line in the Great Hall to receive, and have a look at, their young mistress; how shy I did feel with all their eyes upon me and how glad I was to escape upstairs, and how I longed for the morning when I might walk all about and see every hole and corner of my new home. It was very different then to what it is now and the Great Hall did indeed look as it might have done in Shakespeare's time, with its old worn paved floor, its small panes of glass in its large oriel window, and every window frame creaking and rattling with every gust of wind; and so cold—oh the cold! No hot air then as now, no beautiful garden in the court—only a few large beds with shrubs and old-fashioned flowers. I soon caused my husband to let me root them all up, and I planned the present one, which is such a pleasure to me.

Even from the very beginning, time never seemed too long with my outdoor amusements and indoor pursuits: music, drawing, reading. My husband, who was in Parliament, often asked me to come and help him with his letters on business, and even sometimes to write them. In short, I became his secretary and he would say to me, 'you are the Mary after my own heart'.

On Christmas Day we went to Charlecote church and words cannot describe my inward thoughts as I prayed to God that I might be ever mindful of my duty as a wife, and be diligent in the discharge of such duties as His providence should allot me. I sadly missed the fine organ and choir of St Asaph Cathedral. Our music was a bassoon and a few voices, mostly out of tune. The little old church itself seemed so poor. It was of Anglo-Norman origin but not one architectural beauty remained. It consisted simply of a nave and a chancel, nearly the whole space of the latter was filled by three magnificent monuments to three Sir Thomas Lucys—the builder of the house and his son and grandson, who lived through the reigns of Queen Elizabeth and James 1st. After the service we walked back across the park, beautiful in the winter sunshine, the deer coming quite close to us, seeming unafraid.

Our first visitor was Lord Willoughby de Broke, a near

neighbour, and how little did I realise that such an old fogey (as I thought him) would ever be my brother-in-law! Soon after Christmas—my first not spent among my brothers and sisters—Lord and Lady Warwick, Lady Caroline Greville and Lord and Lady Clonmell called to wish us many Happy New Years in our married life. I was upstairs when I saw their coach and four handsome brown horses with postilions drive into the court, and my heart fluttered with shyness as I rushed down to the drawing room to greet them. But they were all so cordial and pleasant that they soon put me at my ease. The Warwicks were ever after my best neighbours and friends. She had a sweet, pretty face but a bad figure, short and inclined to fat. Lord Warwick was tall and very aristocratic looking.

On the 10th of January I received in a letter from Brother the sad intelligence of the death of poor David Pennant's wife, Lady Caroline, in childbirth. She had a daughter, who survived. How my heart bled for the dear friend of my childhood, her husband, losing after a year and a half's happiness, his gentle, young and lovely wife. My mother wrote to me:

'My dearest Mary, I should have felt keenly disappointed had your situation in life turned out contrary to my expectations, so I may be allowed to indulge in heartfelt gratification on the receipt of every letter that arrives from Charlecote testifying the domestic bliss that already reigns there. Old Nurse came in to hear your letter, her apron up to her eyes, wiping away tears of delight which were chasing each other down her furrowed cheeks at the mention of her dear Mrs Lucy's happenings.

The severe affliction of poor David Pennant weighs us all down. His situation brings before one that of Prince Leopold and the death, in similar circumstances, of his royal Princess.* Lady Caroline was a Princess to her husband and elevated him into a sphere of grandees, yet made him her

*Charlotte, the daughter of George IV who had died in childbed in 1817.

idol. He was in expectation of a son and heir when, after hope had cheered him with the prospect of his wife's recovery, she is snatched away from him and he is left a wretched widower, his estate strictly entailed upon his little daughter. I feel most sincerely for the poor Duchess; she used to say that in Caroline was centred all her happiness.'

On the 29th of March, George (as I shall now call my husband) and I went to Weston to the Clonmells to meet the Warwicks and had a most agreeable visit. We had dancing every evening. I was devoted to Terpsichore but had made a vow when I married to give up my favourite amusement; indeed very few married ladies ever thought of dancing at balls but sat like good mothers watching their daughters dance (but now the mothers dance and even *waltz*, whilst the poor daughters often sit and look on and do not enjoy themselves).

Lord Clonmell was very pressing that I should waltz with him (it was then the rage) and I kept refusing. George laughed and said, 'Come Mary, I absolve you, so, Clonmell, waltz away with her.'

I readily did as my husband bid me and was whisked round and round till I was so giddy I cried out, 'Oh! Let me down or I shall fall,' but he would not stop and it ended with us both nearly falling in the fire. Lady Clonmell was the perfection of grace and beauty, her lord was quite the reverse, burly and noisy with the reddest nose I ever saw, but so good-natured and a capital dancer. He had been George's friend at Harrow and remained so all his life.

One night during this visit Lady Warwick said she would make us all play at 'blind man's buff'. We thought what fun it would be so all the chairs and tables were moved on one side and we all stood up ready for the game. Lord Warwick was the first to be blindfolded and he was a fine long time before he could catch anybody, but at last everyone was caught but me. I was too quick for them. Lady Warwick said, 'Oh! But you shall and must be caught, and I will give a sovereign to any three gentlemen who will undertake to catch you.' So my naughty husband said he would, and Lord Clonmell and Lord Brooke said they would. These three were accordingly blind-folded and I was placed in the middle of the room and Lady Warwick said, 'One, two, three and away!' and all the three put out their arms to catch me. But I, who was very slight and nimble, ran in and out amongst the chairs and tables till I tired them all. Once, my only chance of escape was to jump over a sofa, so I made a spring and cleared it but lost one of my shoes and was obliged to run about without it. Lady Warwick got so excited that she could not resist catching hold of my dress as I passed her, and, it being a muslin one, she tore it but could not stop me. I laughed and said, 'Well, you must give me a new one,' and they all cried out 'Yes! Yes! You deserve one.' The three gentlemen sat down, and said I had fairly beaten them, and I was so tired I had not a leg to stand on so I was glad they gave up. Next morning before I was dressed Lady Clonmell came into my room with about 20 yards of a beautiful pale pink satin for a dress with Lady Warwick's love to me.

Once the young couple were fairly settled in, the ladies of Boddle-wyddan descended on them. Mamma, Emma, Miggy and Old Nurse (who was full of amazement at everything she saw, particularly at the great size of the elms in the avenue, going round them with a tape measure to measure their girth). Mary Elizabeth's sisters returned home full of Charlecote and Sir John wrote off to his favourite daughter, offering her a Boddlewyddan heifer for her dairy, and sheep to run in the park to provide George with the Welsh mutton he so enjoyed.

'My dearest Mary, I think of you and Mr Lucy every day and pray for the happiness of you both night and day. Any man with money can build a new house but an old respected mansion like Charlecote that is above price can only be found in the possession of the first families; and I hope this little pain in the tooth that I hear of is the forerunner of a long line of Lucys . . .'

In his young wife George found a temperament that was opposite to his own. Where he was often low-spirited and prone to misgivings she was all openness and strength. At the wedding he had stood by in dismay, helpless, while she was revived from her fainting fit. As life went on, she learnt to make the decisions for both of them. She was so ready to learn that it was happiness for him to train her taste in painting and sculpture, while she undertook his musical education. Writing years later she was to say:

> 'I often communed with my heart and strove to forget how I had loved and been loved, and then at last my whole life became as fondly devoted to my husband as if he had been the object of my earliest affection.'

★   ★   ★

In April (1824) we went to Compton Verney, Lord Willough-by de Broke's house, taking Miggy, and spent two pleasant days. The old Lord did his best to entertain us. Miggy thought the place charming and inferred that she would rather like to be its mistress.

Later that month we took a house in London for the Season, 10 Upper Grosvenor Street. The servants and the four carriage and riding horses went up and we followed the next day. On the 16th of May George was obliged to return to Charlecote as the Yeomanry were called out on duty for a week. We had not been parted before and I was miserable, especially as I was to be presented on the 20th by Lady Warwick (and Miggy by Lady Harriett Williams-Wynne).

What excitement and fuss there was dressing for our presentation at Court! I thought dear Miggy looked simple perfection in her robe and train of white silk and feathers and lappets and she thought me the same. We only wished George could see us. My dress was the one brought from Lyons for the sister who married first, of white tulle covered with small silver stars, and round the skirt flowers worked in shades of lilac, the

underneath petticoat was of white satin, and the train too of
the richest white satin trimmed with a broad blond lace and
edged with a thick silver cord. On my head a plume of ostrich
feathers, blond lappets and diamonds. On my neck the large
ruby (in form of a heart) with diamond centre, and my
splendid diamond earrings worn for the first time.

I took Miggy to St James's Square to go with Lady Harriett
Williams-Wynne, and then went to Seymour Place, my heart
fluttering and beating like a bird newly caged. I was ushered
into the drawing room where a party of grandees, the Marquis of Hertford (with the Garter), etc., were assembled to look
at and admire or criticise each other. The carriages were then
announced and the Warwicks took me with them. It did not
take long to get to St James's Palace as Lady Warwick, who
was a great favourite of George IV, had the private entrée.*
Then, having passed through several rooms, I stood before the
King who sat upon his royal throne and was clothed with all
his robes of majesty—and Oh! how I trembled as I heard my
name called out. The King stooped down and kissed my cheek
and I know not what I did, but as I was about to move away he
stopped me and said, 'What is your name? I did not catch it.' So
the Lord Chamberlain in a loud voice cried out, 'Mrs Lucy'.
The King then gave me a most gracious smile and allowed me
to go, and I was too glad and thankful to hide my blushes and
confusion and get away.

When Lord Warwick's carriage drew up to take us home, a
gentleman (whose name I forget) said to me, 'Your splendid
ruby which I could not help noticing just now is gone.'

'Oh!' I exclaimed. 'How could it have got unhooked? What
shall I do?' The kindly gentleman volunteered to go at once
and search for it. I was obliged to go as Lord and Lady
Warwick were in the carriage calling out for me. As I was in
the act of getting in, holding up my train, what was my frantic
joy to spy the beautiful ruby hooked in the lace. Oh! How I

*She had been his mistress.

seized it, and how the dear Warwicks participated in my happiness.

Three days later dear George returned and that same evening we all went to a ball at Lord Willoughby de Broke's, 21 Hill Street, Berkeley Square, given by his sister, the Honble Mrs Barnard, whose only daughter had just come out. They always made Lord Willoughby de Broke's house in London their own in the Season. It was a very good ball and fine company, and Miggy enjoyed herself greatly. Curious that her first London ball should take place in a house that was to be her own and that our next ball was in Dover Street at Lady Maria Stanley's, whose second son, about my age, was hereafter to be the husband of my dear sister Ellin. This week was a fearful one of dissipation: four balls, concerts, the play, dinners and parties every night.

The next week *we* gave two dinners. We had a most accomplished artist, Sharp, as cook, equal to any man. She had an aunt who was housekeeper to the King and every third or seventh year (I forget which) she had as her prerequisite all the Royal table linen. Through Sharp, she offered us for £50 thirty of the finest Holland damask tablecloths very little the worse for wear. Of course we readily gave the £50, there never was such a bargain!

Our last ball was at the Honble Mrs West's. Miggy had had dancing to her heart's content and I was heartily weary of London and all its gaieties, and longed for the quiet of the country. We returned to dear Charlecote on the 16th. It was a wonderful joy to be at home again. Every creature, every flower seemed to welcome me, my heart was singing and dancing every moment of the day.

My dear parents, Sister, Ellin and Old Nurse came again to visit us and my happiness knew no bounds. Then on the 10th September (1824), the very day after our return from Warwick Races, my first son, my most precious William Fulke, came into the world, to leave it again in the flower of his age. I caught cold from the monthly nurse taking me out for a ride too soon and I was ill for months and suffered fearfully with a gathered breast. Darling Mamma remained with me till October, then was obliged to return to my father, and left Sister with me. I nursed my baby till the end of November when Mr Hodgson, a clever surgeon from Birmingham, was called in, as I continued so very weak and ill. He at once desired me to wean the little pet.

On the 29th of December, George, Sister, the dear baby and I set off for Boddlewyddan and arrived there on the following day. It was not until February that I was able to go to church and receive the Holy Communion, and with what a grateful heart I entered the old cathedral and knelt at the altar, no longer a trembling bride but a happy mother.

Her parents saw with delight that their daughter was well and happily married, yet felt that some admonishment would not be out of place. Sir John wrote:

'As you are now a steady housewife remember what I told you respecting all orders at shops. Never allow anyone to give or accept an order that is not in writing, let you or your housekeeper do this and do you inspect her books every week and settle them every month. You will then have full command of your household. For the wages Mr Lucy gives, you ought to have a first class gardener who will produce for you plenty of fruit and have it sent up to you in London where it will be extravagantly dear. My dear Mary, excuse my saying this but you are young and anxiety for your welfare dictates it.'

Brought up frugally and with respect for money, Mary Elizabeth was not as likely to overspend as was her husband. His love of the place and of rare and beautiful objects was leading him on to project massive improvements to Charlecote and to spend a great deal of money on the Dutch and Italian masters which he meant to hang on its walls. As a Member of Parliament he had to have a London house for the Session.

40

In the spring George again went up to London and took a house, 15 Grosvenor Place, and the servants and horses etc. went up, and then Baby and I. Darling Baby was put in short clothes and Ellin came for two nights when I had to take her back to school in Eaton Place, but Sister came to us for the Season.

I shall only mention one event that Season, which I can *never* forget, a ball at Lord Heneker's. We had not been long in the room, and I was standing alone, George having left me to speak to a friend in the adjoining room, when I caught sight of Wilson Patten whom I had not met since our parting two years before. He had only just returned from abroad and had not heard of my marriage. He soon saw me and his hand was clasped in mine, he must have felt it tremble. I strove to suppress my emotion, I almost gasped for breath. He looked at my costly dress and diamonds, and almost shrieked, 'I see I have lost you, you are no longer my own dear sweet Mary, and my happiness is gone for ever,' and he rushed out of the room, and I believe left London for I saw him no more. When George joined me I felt so faint and ill that I asked him to call for our carriage and take me home, which he did, and then I told him how dearly I had loved Wilson Patten and was beloved, before I had known him and become his wife, but added, 'Now you hold my heart and soul. But I must ever love and esteem one who was so dear to me, ere I ever saw you.'

His hand was on my shoulder, I felt its touch was kind, he smiled and said, 'I have no jealous fears. I fully trust you, my dearest Mary.'

When we returned to Charlecote, Mrs Lucy, George's mother, came to stay; it was the first time we had met. She was a dear kind old lady, taking me to her heart from the moment she saw me, cherishing me as her own daughter, divesting herself of all her jewels, her pearls and fine old lace to adorn her 'own dear darling' as she used to call me. She then lived at Bath, but eventually lived here and died here. She remained with us till near the end of the year when we went to visit my family at Boddlewyddan.

How happy I was then, wandering over all my old haunts, my little garden, the little cottage with its cockleshells etc. And to sit with dear Old Nurse and read her a chapter out of the Bible and trim up her caps; and how devoted the good old soul was to my baby boy. After Christmas, George was obliged to go to London to attend his Parliament duties and I was to return home from Boddlewyddan the week before my confinement, which I expected in March. 'But man proposes and God disposes.' On the 1st February, I was sitting copying some music in Mamma's boudoir whilst she was working and chatting, when all of a sudden we heard the report of a gun, and she got up and went to the window which looked out upon the lawn, pulled down the blind and rushed out of the room. I jumped up feeling something must be wrong, and drawing up the blind, saw to my horror Brother flat on his face with his gun beside him. I hurried downstairs in an agony of fright, and fainted ere I could learn what had happened. Dear Mamma, like me, thought he had been shot, and after all he had lain down on the grass to watch a ferret come out of a rabbit hole!

That night I was taken very ill, and at one o'clock in the morning a daughter was born, and old Nurse was got out of bed to take the precious infant and wrap her in flannel, as all my baby clothes were at Charlecote. However, the next day Mrs Maddox of Glangywern sent me a supply till those at home were sent. I was so delighted to have a girl, but in a terror lest she might not live, she was such a wee thing. I nursed her myself, and would hardly let her be taken out of my arms. I returned home in March with my two dear children. Hugh came with me and we arrived at Charlecote on the 15th, when my husband arrived too from London, bringing Ellin from school. He was charmed with his little daughter. There had been no Miss Lucy since Elizabeth, the only child of Captain Thomas Lucy and his beautiful wife Catherine, born in 1670.

In June, Ellin left school for good and came here. We did not take a house in London that season as I was not very strong, but we had much company at home, and dearest Mamma and some of my sisters and brothers were generally staying here. George was always so kind to my relations.

In August, George went with me to Birmingham to consult Mr Hodgson about me, and, as I was still nursing my darling Mary Emily, she had to accompany us. In returning in our carriage (a chaise) with our own four horses and postilions, a terrific thunderstorm came on, the sky seemed ablaze with fire, the lightning was very blue and forked and flash succeeded flash with the utmost rapidity, and the noise of the thunder made the earth tremble. We were in an agony of terror, thinking every moment either ourselves, servants or horses would be struck. The dear baby, who was on my knee (her nurse was outside with the footman) unconscious of the danger, was crowing at the bright light. George was just pulling down the blinds to hide, if possible, the fearful blaze, when the horses all of a sudden stood still as if they had been struck, and we saw a ball of fire fall within a hundred yards of us, on the other side of the hedge. We fell back in the carriage electrified with shock. We were then about two miles on this side of Warwick. The horses would not move on for several minutes. The storm continued till some time after we reached home. George went next day to see the spot where the thunderbolt had fallen; he found the earth torn up and a large hole, but no mineral substance, though he had a man dig very deep hoping to find some trace of it.

In September of that year Mr Wilson Patten came to Charlecote. He had been staying at Sherborne near by and my husband asked him to spend some days with us, which gave me great pleasure. The day after his arrival George proposed our all three riding to Warwick, so after luncheon we started, without a groom. When we got to Warwick my husband said to me, 'I have some business to do, so please stop here in High Street until I join you.' We waited two whole hours when I got quite alarmed and thought he must have had an accident, so we cantered away as fast as possible for home, but just before we reached the village my pony stumbled and rolled over on me. I was so hurt that when the pony got up and I tried to do the same, I fainted. When I came to myself, Mr W. P. was kneeling by me and I heard him say, 'Dearest Mary. Oh, my dearest Mary.' I got up and said 'Do get your horse and my pony' (which were quietly feeding close to the road) 'and help me to mount,' which he did. I could hardly sit in the saddle I was in such pain. He said 'I trust you are not much hurt?' and we neither of us spoke again.

The instant I got home I asked a footman if Mr Lucy had come back and the answer was, 'Yes, long ago.' So I rushed, as well as I was able, upstairs and told him what had occurred and asked him what he meant by bidding us stay in Warwick till he joined us, and then never came. He looked displeased and told me to get dressed as some of our expected guests had already arrived (we had a dinner party). I said 'I am in such pain I don't think I can come down to dinner.' However, I obeyed him, and was in misery all the evening. As soon as he came up to bed, and I had dismissed my maid, I kissed him and said, 'Surely you are not jealous? You have no cause, you cannot suppose that I would have stayed in Warwick if you had not desired me to do so. You know how I love you and would not cause you a moment's uneasiness.' He listened with visible emotion and pressed me to his heart. But I never could make out the mystery of his leaving us.

In May, Brother, George and I left Charlecote for Leyton Grange, Mr John Lane's. We slept at Salt Hill and got to the Grange the following evening when there was a very gay ball to celebrate his pretty wife's coming of age; and there I met Mr Disraeli (the late Lord Beaconsfield) who no one could have foretold would have become Prime Minister and so great a man. I thought him in appearance an insignificant looking person and quite a fop with his black corkscrew curls, and his Jewish nose.

From the Lanes we went to London. George had taken 39 Bryanston Square, a very large house, and beautifully furnished, for which he paid 500 guineas for the Season. It was charming for the dear children as the rooms were so spacious and airy. I was so happy to have Brother to ride with me in the Park and go to the opera, etc., with me, for George never cared to go and I never would go alone.

I recall that it was during this visit that I was introduced to the Countess of Cork. She was dressed in white satin and had a little white satin hat on her old head. She never could go out without carrying off something, and when she dined out she regularly put as many silver spoons and forks as she could in her pocket. The next morning a servant was sent to get them back. I was told a capital story of her. She was on a visit to the Archbishop of York, and his daughters determined to play her a trick when she was going away. Their father had a pet hedgehog and this creature they wrapped up in a shawl and placed it in the hall, feeling sure that she would covet the shawl and carry it off, and so it came to pass, for after she said, 'Goodbye my dears,' they saw her whip up the shawl and take it into her carriage. As she drove through York she unfolded the shawl and to her dismay found the Archbishop's pet hedgehog. She immediately put down the window and bid the driver stop at the first pastry cook's shop, which he did, and the chief baker, seeing a coronet carriage at his door, flew out to know what her ladyship wanted, so she said, 'Bring me a tray with some of your nicest cakes.' So he brought her what she desired. She took the tray into the carriage through the window, emptied all the cakes into her lap and tossed the Archibishop's hedgehog on the tray to the man, and cried out, 'Drive on,' and the chief baker to his astonishment found a hedgehog and no money, and all his nice cakes gone.

We were quite as gay this season as the last—balls, concerts, dinners out and dinners at home, but on July 7th I was taken ill of what was then called a 21 days low fever. I was attended by the fashionable physician, Dr Warren, who took snuff in such a quantity that when he felt my pulse I was covered with it, and he would sit often for half an hour by my bed, talking and sniffing pinch after pinch up his nose till he made me quite sick and I wished him at Jericho. I was not well enough to be moved for five long weeks.

Soon after I was taken ill Brother left us and I received the following amusing letter from him dated September 4th 1827, Pippins Rectory.

'My dearest Mary, I was more than delighted to receive your last charming letter. I have flown about at all rates this year, and have to thank Lucy and yourself for the pleasantest part of my ramble, which it was certain to be under your roof and in your kind company. I am now staying in a very old and cold Rectory with very high bred agreeable people who suffer the mortifications of poverty the more from having true notions and ideas of style, the bearings and manners of grandees, with the cooking and bedding of beggars. Mr Cathcart is so connected with military men and diplomatists that he is very little of the clergyman, even on a Sunday. It is a singular circumstance that both his father, Lord Cathcart, and his brother, the present Lord, were ambassadors at St Petersburg. Mr Cathcart knew the Empress Catherine when a boy and his anecdotes of her Court are very amusing. MC's three sisters married greatly—the Duchess of Atholl, the Countess of Mansfield and Lady Lynedoch. Mr Cathcart has the ease and agreeableness of a man of the world. He is a very near relation of Lord Warwick's. You will think my heart stood a good siege when I tell you there are seven Miss Cathcarts! I am a little singed by Miss Charlotte, a most agreeable girl. They dress very well and are very accomplished and unaffected. Good night my dearest Mary, your ever affectionate brother, John Williams.'

Caroline, second daughter and third child of George and Mary Elizabeth, was born in January 1828, and again it was a difficult birth. The baby was small and delicate and grew up to be a fair replica of her mother in stature and colouring, but without the vivacity. Her life was to be short and tragic, but she was happily married and withstood the dangers of India with great courage.

The children and garden had now become too absorbing to allow of more than brief mentions of parties and visits in the journals. On the first morning after Mary Elizabeth's arrival at Charlecote she had found nettles growing waist-high in the wilderness which Capability Brown had planted with Scotch pine and surrounded with sculptured hedges of box and yew. Now the dense undergrowth had gone and the wild flowers she had planted carpeted the ground. She was disappointed that lilies would not thrive even though George brought back pulverised sea-shells from his Cornish constituency to encourage them. But briar roses and honeysuckle, her two favourite flowers, enlaced the tree trunks.

In the same month that Caroline was born, Charlecote received a very distinguished visitor. Mary Elizabeth describes the occasion with characteristic enthusiasm.

In January, Sir Walter Scott and his daughter Ann paid old Charlecote a visit, so early that we were in bed and were awoke by the ringing of the front door bell; and don't I remember our hurry to get dressed when we heard *who* it was that had arrived and were waiting for permission to see the house!

When we went down he and Miss Scott were intently surveying the pictures in the Great Hall. I see him now in my mind's eye (fifty years or more later), advancing to meet us with the most genuine expression of benevolence and shrewd humour in his face, his hair white as snow and his eyebrows very thick and shaggy, his crippled foot giving him a limping gait. He remained with us about two hours; he made me play him some Welsh airs, he seemed delighted with the place, but he was pressed for time, alas, and could not stay longer. He would fain have spent some days with us. This short visit, however, stamped us friends and we parted with the hope and promise of his coming here again and of our visiting Abbotsford.

Sir Walter also recorded the visit, describing Charlecote as 'the abode of ease and opulence. There were some fine old books and I was told of more that were not in order. How odd if a folio Shakespeare should be found amongst them. This visit gave me great pleasure, it really brought Justice Shallow before my eyes!' (Shakespeare had reputedly taken his revenge on Sir Thomas Lucy, the Justice of the Peace, by holding him up to ridicule as Justice Shallow in 'The Merry Wives of Windsor'.)

That autumn dear Miggy came to us and stayed the whole winter and on her account we were very gay. Miggy's hopes were high as the old Lord endeavoured to show her some attention. He invited us to Compton Verney and we accepted and stayed the old year out and the New Year in. Then in mid-January Lord Willoughby came to Charlecote for the hunt ball at Stratford. At the ball he sat by me and, our conversation turning on matrimony, I said to him, 'Why don't you take a wife?'

'Oh, no nice girl would take such an old fellow as me.'

I said, 'Faint heart never won fair lady. Take my advice and try.'

The next day he left Charlecote and I got the most ridiculous letter from him, asking if I thought he had any chance of winning my sister. I showed Miggy the letter and said, 'What answer shall I send? Remember he is old enough to be your father and you cannot be in love with him. It may be all very fine to be Lady Willoughby de Broke but a coronet will not ensure your happiness.'

George, too, spoke very seriously to her but all cautioning was vain. She determined to be mistress of Compton Verney, so my answer to him was 'You had better come and ask her yourself.' He came and she accepted him, with delightful anticipation of the future. You cannot imagine the surprise and the talk this marriage occasioned. His daughter, Mrs Barnard (who had made a *mésalliance* with her son's tutor—her son was heir to the title and estate) was furious. Lord Willoughby it struck me was rather afraid of entering the Holy Estate of matrimony. He stayed at Charlecote till the end of January, his love-making was very mild; no lover's vows 'sweet in every whisper'd word'. Then he went to Boddlewyddan to meet my parents, taking his lawyer with him to make the necessary settlements, and we took Miggy to London to get her trousseau. Lord Willoughby gave me *carte blanche* to buy her whatever jewels she wished and her wedding veil, and I did not spare his money! George and I gave her a very handsome brooch and earrings, but neither she nor her rich old Peer gave us the smallest acknowledgement for all the expense we had been put to.

On the 3rd of March she was married by special licence in the Cathedral at St Asaph by the Bishop. They came back to Boddlewyddan as Lord and Lady Willoughby de Broke to luncheon and to have their healths drunk, and after it went to Lord Bagot's Poole Park for simply one night and then set off for Compton Verney.

There were twenty-seven years between their ages: he was the fifth richest man in England. There were to be no children, but the marriage was not unhappy for he had taken a wife who dedicated herself to ensuring his comfort. Compton Verney became a second home to Mary Elizabeth and her children. The Barnards had no cause for alarm; their son eventually inherited and ran through his uncle's fortune. In the now ruined chapel of Compton Verney, Margaret Willoughby de Broke's monument bears the simple words 'Blessed are the pure in heart'.

'Well and happy' is the only comment in the journal when, after a three weeks' interval, the Lucys dined at Compton Verney with the bridal pair.

Dark Leaves in the Wreath

Driving back from her sister's wedding Mary Elizabeth's view of the old house, hitherto so uncritically loved and admired, suffered a change of perception sharpened by unadmitted envy of her sister. Compton Verney, built by Robert Adam and lavishly landscaped by Capability Brown, was a nobleman's seat, and as such was illustrated in volumes of 'Mansions of England' and 'Seats of the Nobility and Gentry'. By contrast Charlecote was undeniably shabby with its Tudor brickwork damaged in places by a stucco wash applied in the previous century. Her deep affection for the place was not to be allowed to get in the way of her practical good sense. For one thing there was urgent need for the latest improvement in water closets (two earth closets situated in turrets at opposite ends of the house served the whole household).

A builder's survey had revealed grave defects in the fabric. The wainscoting of the Great Hall was worm-eaten in places, the Minstrels' Gallery and the oak screen that supported it were pronounced to be only fit for firewood. Sir Walter Scott had inadvertently fired George with the idea of a hall like that at Abbotsford, painted to simulate stone with a frieze of deer's antlers and a library with a gallery running round it for the use of those who wished to while away an afternoon browsing on books. Parcels of books from Pickering in Chancery Lane had been arriving for some time. Purchases that George had made when a bachelor from the sale in 1822 of William Beckford's collection at Fonthill were still waiting to be unpacked.

Also he was in treaty with Buchanan, a London art dealer, for the purchase of Dutch and Italian masters.

It all proved to be far more of an undertaking than they had lightheartedly supposed. When the first hole gaped where a window had been, letting in more cold air than had ever been felt by Mary Elizabeth when she wrote that her new home was 'cold, oh! so cold!', George was dismayed. The stained glass put up after the Queen's visit had to be taken down piece by piece and some of it got broken. He would have been frantic had not his wife, always able to extract fun from a situation, calmed him and found a solution. One of his farm houses was without a tenant: they would furnish it and stay there, visiting the rebuilding every day to inspect progress until the house was fit to be lived in again. It would be like a second honeymoon, for the children, now three in number, would go to Boddlewyddan.

It was not to be so simple. Two rooms were to be built out towards the river on the west side, a library and a dinner room. They would have book shelves, flock wallpapers, Tudor-style plaster ceilings and much wood carving in the Tudor fashion on door handles, shelves and door casings.

To be fair to these early Victorian Lucys the house was in bad repair; simply to save it from further decay would have been a sufficiently lengthy undertaking, but (as they would have put it) to beautify and embellish it was going to take almost seven years.

Heraldry, with special reference to his own descent, was George's passion. He had taught himself the elementary rules, but in heraldry every rule subdivides. He needed someone far more knowledgeable than he was to learn from, and found that someone in an architect-craftsman, Thomas Willement, Stained-Glass Artist to George IV, who was called in to repair the damaged Tudor glass. Willement was deeply versed in the lore of heraldry. George had it in mind to introduce more heraldic glass into his new rooms, and indeed wherever space could be found for it. The tall bay window in the Great Hall contained ancient painted glass that set out the descent of the Charle-cote Lucys through a twelfth-century marriage with a daughter of one of the Lords Lucy of Cockermouth (a barony that passed to the Northumberlands). No one doubted that here was the justification for

Justice Shallow's boast that 'a dozen white lucies do become an old coat well,' for in these shields was the family emblem plain to be seen—the white pike or luce, which is the Lucy emblem, many times repeated. By the time George died the luce would be everywhere at Charlecote: on carpets, on tiles, in embroidery; carved, printed, painted, engraved.

While George and Mary Elizabeth realised that the rebuilding of Charlecote would disrupt their domestic peace and congenial routine for some time to come, naturally they did not foresee what shadows were to gather round their sunny hearth. Until now Mary Elizabeth had never encountered the chill presence of death, even among those who were not close to her. When the spectre arrived, it remained, its shadows hovering close among them, its eye alert for every opportunity. It seemed that a sombre and harrowing battle was being waged, for each death that came was matched, as though in compensation, by a birth. Happiness and sorrow were indeed, as she had put it, twined together. During these years Mary Elizabeth's naturally buoyant nature and firm religious faith enabled her spirit to conquer its overwhelming distress. Not so with George.

The first of these sad events, the death of Sir John Williams of Boddlewyddan, occurred in the autumn of 1830.

I was walking across the Park to see some of the poor people in the village when I saw my brother Hugh getting over the paling and coming to meet me. I instantly thought he was the messenger of bad news from Boddlewyddan. He endeavoured to prepare me in vain, so at length he told me that our dearest father had died the previous night after an illness of 24 hours. I was overcome with grief and shock. Lord Willoughby and dear Margaret made us, with our children, go at once to Compton that we might weep together and they most kindly insisted on our remaining for my confinement as, of course, we could not now go to Wales. So we accepted and on Sunday the 28th November 1830 at two o'clock our second son, Henry Spencer, was born. I shall here transcribe part of a letter from my mother written soon after dearest father's death.

'My dearest Mary, no consolation to me is so great as conversing with my only comforts and writing to my absent ones, my beloved children. My days have been unclouded from my birth but my loss is so great that time alone can soften feelings that now bow me down. When I am with your dear brothers and sisters I support myself wonderfully, but when they leave me and the silence of night surrounds me and I look round for the partner of my life—from whom for the length of years I have ever been accustomed to have had the greatest kindness and affection—gone for ever, then I feel the desolation of widowhood. My dearest Mary, I well know that a few lines from me will be the greatest comfort to you as your kind letters were to me. I have been 39 years without knowing trouble but my affliction is now a heavy one and had not the Almighty sent me such comforters as my children I must have sunk under it. The past is like a shadow but the image is so engraven upon my heart that it is never absent. I cherish everything that belonged to him who was my support for so many years.'

It was not until the following autumn, nearly a year later, that George, our four children and I set off on the two day journey for Boddlewyddan. As I approached the home of my childhood with a sad yearning heart how my thoughts flew back to that loving greeting with which my dearest father always welcomed me, and now he would no longer be at the door to watch for our coming. His death was the first great sorrow in my hitherto happy life, but alas, 'Life needs dark leaves in the wreath'.

Soon after our arrival we were invited to Sir Richard Bulkely's Baron Hall. Fourteen years had fled like a dream since I, then a child, had been at Baron Hall with my parents. On this occasion, Brother, Emma, Ellin and I met there Lady Maria Stanley, her son William Owen and three daughters, besides many more. William Owen Stanley fell desperately in love with Ellin—and Ellin with him—so on the 19th the Stanleys came to Brother's. The ladies only staid [sic] for a couple of days but William Owen Stanley stopped and accompanied us, with Brother, Emma and Ellin, to the Glyns at Hawarden Castle, and there after so short a courtship he asked Ellin to be his wife and she said yes. There was great rejoicing and endless congratulations. (The two Miss Glyns, Sir Stephen's sisters, were beautiful girls. The eldest is the present Mrs Gladstone, wife of the Prime Minister.) Dear Ellin was married in February (from Boddlewyddan) in the parish church of St Aspah, and they were the happiest couple possible.

That spring the heat was excessive and I remember sitting out in the court watching the gardener planting out the verbenas. Lord Frederic and Lady Augusta FitzClarence and their pretty little daughter, Mary FitzClarence, came to luncheon and staid for an early dinner (as they were at Leamington). I was so fatigued entertaining them that I was taken ill soon after they left, and continued in much suffering the whole night of Sunday, all Monday, till eleven o'clock on Tuesday night, when Herbert Almeric was born, to be taken at four years old to a better world.

The prescribed period of mourning for a parent was almost as lengthy as was mourning for a husband. After a year, grey or mauve with deep bands of black crepe on the sleeves and hem was de rigueur for the children as for the parents. No jewellery was permissible in the first year except mourning rings, brooches and bracelets with the hair of the deceased, but in the second year amethysts and moonstones might be worn. Mary Elizabeth does not dwell on her sorrow since the journals are written for her grandchildren's amusement, but the first note of sadness, forecast of the tragic losses to come, is felt. Ellin's happiness is a deep comfort as is the joy of a new baby, but she was not to be able to modify the heavy black that convention decreed: word now came that her mother was very ill.

On 14th February, 1843, having a bad account of dearest Mamma, the Stanleys, Baby and I started off for Cheltenham. Oh what agony! As soon as I arrived, and before I could get out of the carriage, Sister and Emma came and said 'Mary, it is of no use getting out of the carriage for our dear Mother is far too ill to see you tonight, you can come early in the morning.' I burst into tears, and declared I could not, *would* not go away without seeing her. Then her good maid Davies, who was very fond of me, came and remonstrated with my sisters and said she knew her dear mistress would see me and that I must not go to the hotel, as she would have a room got ready directly for me and Baby.

So Sister had to give way and I jumped out of the carriage, flew upstairs and on tip toe went into my angel Mamma's bedroom. In a moment she saw me and said, 'Oh! My darling Mary, how glad I am to see you. I am very, very ill, but the very sight of you does me good. And where is my god child? Send for him!' So Baby was brought and put on her bed, and he was so good, and she kissed him and blessed him.

She died on the 21st of February and I lost the loved one of my soul, the light of my days. And now both my beloved parents were gone to the higher and better world, and my tears and despair could not recall them to life. I sobbed forth a prayer that I might die the death of the righteous and see them again to part no more. But the loss and the sadness of death are balanced by the joy and renewal of birth and six months after dearest Mamma's death, Reginald Aymer was born at nine o'clock a.m.

My husband had got up very early to shoot a buck. I had been ill for some hours and told him perhaps he would find a little stranger when he came back, but he laughed and said 'nonsense', and great was his surprise when he had killed the deer and returned to find he had a fourth son. I got over my confinement very well for the first month, but afterwards suffered so from neuralgia in my head and face that I was ordered a change of air, and so with Baby I went to stay with Brother at Boddlewyddan.

While we were there the Duke of Sussex, who was staying at Kinmel, came over with Lord Dinorben to shoot and dine at Boddlewyddan. My dear old Nurse, who was still living with Brother and darning his stockings, had such a wish to see a royal duke that Brother said she must put on her best silk gown and lace ruff, etc., and she should come in at dessert; so, when the bell rang for her, she appeared and Brother gave her a glass of wine and, making the lowest curtsey to the duke, she drank his health, wishing him all possible good health and happiness. He was charmed with her—shook hands with her and, filling his glass, drank her good health in a bumper. So the dear old soul, making another low curtsey, left the room as proud as a peacock. Not long afterwards she died at Boddlewyddan and was buried close to my dear parents at the Cathedral of St Asaph. Beloved and respected by us all, she had lived in our family 45 years. I had a charming miniature by Hargreaves done of her when I married, and I always look at it with the most affectionate pleasure, and almost fancy I can hear her speak, it is such an admirable likeness. Hargreaves did miniatures at the same time of me, dearest Papa, Mamma and my four sisters, for which I paid him 10 guineas each.

In March I weaned dear Aymer. Hugh and Emma came to us and on the 5th of April he was christened in Charlecote Church by John Lucy. His sponsors were the Bishop of St Asaph, Lord Brooke and Ellin Stanley. We sat down 20 to dinner.

This dinner was memorable not only for the occasion it celebrated but because for the very first time they were dining in the new dinner room. The fine linen tablecloth with the royal cypher that had once covered the Prince Regent's table at Carlton House was set with a service of silvergilt bought from Rundell and Bridge in 1824, with gold coasters by Paul Storr and silver candelabra by de Lamerie. Hertfords, Warwicks, Willoughby de Brokes were all there; Mary Elizabeth

wearing between her black curls the diamond wheatear ornaments that
George had given her to celebrate the occasion.

Those who had been staying with us for darling Baby's
christening had only just departed when Lord and Lady
Shrewsbury with Prince Doria, on their way to London,
drove over to spend the day with us. We were so sorry that
they had not written to propose themselves to us instead of
going to a village inn. The Prince was in raptures with old
Charlecote, and so admired the large Florentine table in the
Great Hall, which had originally stood in the Borghese Villa at
Rome, and from whence it had been taken by the French in the
time of Napoleon. It was bought by my husband at the sale of
Fonthill for one thousand eight hundred guineas. (The Prince
Borghese had recently married Lord Shrewsbury's youngest
daughter and Prince Doria was engaged to Lady Mary Talbot,
the eldest.)

At luncheon the Prince liked the Charlecote biscuits so
much that I said laughing, 'You must carry some away,' and
so I ordered a packet of them to be put in the carriage. Just after
they had started I saw the packet of biscuits left behind, so I
took it, and ran after the carriage, and I caught them up before
they got through the Park gate, and gave it to the Prince.
When we went to Rome three years after, nothing could
exceed the kindness of Prince Doria and his charming wife,
and he said to me he should never forget my running after him
with the Charlecote biscuits.

Not long after this I went out riding on a bay mare of John
Lucy's. He had asked me to try her as he wanted to sell her to
carry a lady. I took dear little Carry with me on her pony. We
went to Loxley and, returning, the mare tried her best to kick
me off and I tried my best to stick on and just as I thought she
was good and cantering quietly along she suddenly sent her
heels up such a height that I was thrown and, falling on my left
arm, broke every bone in it and dislocated my wrist. I bid the
groom go home and send the carriage for me, and also send for

Mathews, a famous bone setter. I pulled off my wedding ring as my hand was beginning to swell and thought I would try and walk and, gathering up the skirt of my habit, set off, when dear Carry made me laugh by saying, 'Dear Mamma, you are showing your legs so!' However, my legs did not take me far, for I fainted and fell down by the side of the road, where I was found when the carriage with Turner my faithful maid came. Poor Carry was kneeling by me crying bitterly, believing me to be dead.

Mathews did not arrive till midnight and Oh! Heavens, I shudder now at the bare remembrance of the tortures I suffered. For a full 20 minutes he was pulling my arm and wretched wrist by main force into their place, and then bound both so tightly that the blood oozed out of my nails. My husband standing by my bed, exclaiming, 'Oh! My dearest Mary, I shall never hear you play again!' Mathews attended me for six months. He used to pull each finger separately until I fainted with agony, then after a while he would make me hold a wax candle and lastly a pin. He told me it would depend on my own exertions if I ever had the perfect use of my fingers again, that I must not mind pain, but use my hand as much as possible, and so I did and after a few years I could play nearly as well as ever.

★   ★   ★

It was during the Easter holidays in 1839 that our darling Herbert Almeric fell ill with a feverish cold. Dr Thomas and Mr England attended him, but finding he grew worse rather than better we consulted Mr Hodgson of Birmingham who had done me much good in the past but who on feeling his stomach said, 'Dear little fellow, the mischief is here.' Observing how wretched I was, he tried to comfort me by saying that Herbie's constitution was so good that he might recover but we must not expect any improvement for some months. Alas, in spite of all that medical skill and affection could do, he faded away like a broken flower and on Monday the 3rd August 1839 his spirit fled to the God who gave it and the Church bell rang its remorseless tone for him, so young, so beautiful, so good, on whom our very souls doted. He passed away with so calm and sweet a parting it scarcely seemed like death, and there he lay in his little bed, peaceful and lovely as if asleep, in that room that I have lived to call the *fatal* or *death* room, since every child born in it I have lived to mourn the death of.

His poor little body, enclosed in a coffin covered with the finest white silk velvet with silver ornaments (by his Papa's express wish) was borne up the old avenue of elms to its last home in the vault of Charlecote Church by the three sons of Mr Wallington the steward and John Cross, the son of a tenant, followed by his sorrowing father and weeping brothers Fulke and Spencer, and his uncles, Lord Willoughby de Broke, Hugh Williams and John Lucy. I strove hard to say, 'God's will be done,' but it was agony to feel that the object of my care for the four short years of his life was past all help or need of it; that dear little dependent being who I had been accustomed to think of almost every moment of the day, was no longer there to take from my hand his medicine, to listen to the oft-repeated Bible stories or to kneel by my knee and repeat his childish prayers. The rooms he seemed to fill with life, even when his own was waning fast, would know him no more. How these sad events chronicle the advance of Time. A cold weight presses on my heart and the fountain of grief is awakened from its inmost source so that it pains me to write down what I have set out to record.

★   ★   ★

On August 20, 1839, my darling little Edmund Davenport was born. God's gift in His good providence to heal my sore heart. But as the months passed I did not recover my spirits and it was decided that a change of scene would be the best thing for us: his Papa too had been deeply affected. We decided to go abroad, taking our five children with us. There was a sort of sunshine and rain attendant on our going. I liked the thought of Italy and all that there would be to see, but not the prospect of leaving dear Charlecote for perhaps two long years, and leaving every trace of my precious lost Herby. No foreign lands could ever efface his dear image while memory is left to me.

For George there was not the release of ready tears and other woes were added to the loss of his son. In 1832 the Reform Bill had become law and Fowey with the other pocket boroughs had been disfranchised. Westminster knew him no more. While MP for Fowey he had sunk a good deal of money in a Cornish copper mine that failed. The improvements to the house had far outrun the estimates. His political agent in Cornwall had some time earlier offered to take over some tenements which George had been obliged to buy up in order to secure votes. Thirty thousand pounds had been the sum mentioned and George had counted on this to pay the costs of improving Charlecote. The money was not forthcoming. (After George's death the agent did buy the Fowey property—but for much less.)

On the eve of departure a letter came from Buchanan, the picture dealer, saying that he had a buyer who would be prepared to give over three thousand pounds for two paintings; 'I think the sum offered is very large, considering the rate at which you acquired them through me, both the Raphael and the Wouvermans, and I have again to repeat to you, "better to sell and repent than to hold and probably repent".' But George, with the stubbornness of the amateur collector, could not bring himself to part with the paintings, much as he needed the money. He even continued to buy pictures: a very large canvas of St Jerome and the lion by Van Dyke, a Fra Bartolomeo of the Holy Family, a monkey cracking nuts by de Heem, two Pieter de Hoogh interiors, a version (one of the many) of Teniers' Wedding Feast, a Canaletto, another Raphael. He dreamed of a chequered marble floor for the Great Hall, of mantelpieces and mirrors from the Accademia dei Bel Arti in Florence. Italy beckoned, he longed as his forebears had done to gaze on its beauties. But they had not set out encumbered with company other than a subservient secretary to note down their reactions to the scenery. George Lucy was a family man, and the pleasure would have been less without his wife and children to share it. Besides it would be educational for Emily aged fourteen and Carrie aged twelve.

The time was fast approaching for our long-talked-of Continental tour. The last few days before our departure were very sad, taking leave of all we loved. We made Turner housekeeper and I was to hire a foreign maid. My husband, Emily and I quitted dear old Charlecote on the 30th of September and went to Everall's Hotel in Albemarle Street in London. On Monday the 4th of October 1840 the tutor, the Reverend Mr Drake, a courier called Monsieur Desirée, Hughes the nurse, the five children—Fulke, Emily, Caroline, Spencer, Aymer —and the new baby, and Thomas the footman, joined us. We were taking our own two carriages, a coach and a chariot, three beds for the little ones, three tin baths, sheets, towels, pillows, and we had a sort of well fixed under the coach which held lesson books, tea, arrowroot and every possible thing we thought we might need or fancied we might want.

We started that same evening after dinner for the Tower Stairs, it was pouring with rain and my eyes felt very much inclined to do the same. The steam packet, *Sir William Wallace*, was to start to Boulogne at one o'clock in the morning. Nurse and baby were put to bed in a private cabin; Emy and I laid down in the coach and were quite comfortable but not for long as a storm arose and the vessel heaved to and fro, and the waves dashed over and into the carriages and everyone was reeling and staggering and at their wits' end. In short the crossing was terrible and we did not reach Boulogne till four o'clock p.m., having been fourteen hours at sea. We slept at the Hotel des Bains.

At Amiens we stopped to look at the cathedral. Before one of the chapels I observed several farthing rushlights burning and was told that a poor woman had a child ill and that she had offered them for its recovery. I thought of my angel Herby and of the many prayers I had offered for his recovery and I could have wept for her. Alas, how deluded were her notions of God's mercy if she thought that a dozen miserable candles would propitiate in her favour; and yet it was a touching sight.

We arrived in Paris on October the 8th and spent 10 days there sightseeing, all too short. We got to Lyons on the 22nd and there it was that my darling beautiful Edmund Davenport was taken ill. He was the most healthy child and had cut two teeth without any suffering. I was in agony but Desirée tried to comfort me by saying that it was the milk and that it was the case generally with English children and that he would soon be all right, but God willed it otherwise.

The 23rd was a wretched night, my precious baby being convulsed with a violent bowel complaint. The next day I took him into the chaise and carried him all day and watched his every look. He seemed in pain for he flung his little arms about and was very restless. We were determined to get to Turin as quick as possible, hoping there to find medical aid. We wrapped the darling in my flannel dressing-gown and laid him on soft pillows on my lap in the chaise. We began to ascend the Mont Cenis. I thought he was no worse and Mr Lucy even said, 'Mary, I think he is better, your love and care have already done much for him.'

He had not long spoken when we met some rude waggoners and found we were all in danger on account of deep snow in the pass and we had to stop for a considerable time for the men to clear a way; during that time I saw the precious baby was getting rapidly worse, and just as we had crossed Mount Cenis and stopped at Molazetto to change horses he expired in my arms in the chaise. I clasped him to my heart, I drowned him in my tears. I cried to the Lord to have mercy on me, to send his little spirit back to me. My poor husband sprang out of the carriage to fetch Hughes, for I would not let the body out of my sight, and full of grief he went to mourn with the other children in the coach.

Eleven long hours did I travel with his dear lifeless body on my lap ere we reached Turin at three o'clock in the morning.

Never, never can I forget that night of anguish, seated in the carriage with the moon shining bright through the window on that pale but beauteous face—so calm, so still, so lovely in death. At the Hotel Fedor, Turin, with the aid of Hughes, I put the beloved Edmund in a coffin, kissed and kissed again his marble forehead, his lips, his hands; and had it not been for the sake of my dear husband and children still left me, could willingly like David have exclained, 'Oh! My son, my son, that I had died instead of thee!'

In the evening Mr Drake read the funeral service and we all wept and prayed together, and through the kind interference of Mr Abercromby, the British Consul, we were allowed to keep his remains till we could send them back to England. We left Turin on November 2nd and got to Genoa. A Captain Turner, for a considerable sum, agreed to take the remains to England in his brig, the *Matilda*, and when he came and carried off the coffin, to part with it was like parting with a portion of my heart.

The vessel met with many disasters and was more than once nearly wrecked. It did not reach Liverpool till the end of July 1842. On the 23rd November it was brought to Charlecote, put into a coffin covered with white velvet and silver ornaments like dear Herbert's and on the 1st March was laid beside that little brother in the Lucy vault in Charlecote church. John Lucy read the burial service.

'Methinks I hear an angel singing within the golden wall.
'My father! and my gentle mother, attend ye to my call.
  I'm safe at home—more satisfied than I might be on earth;
  Then meet your child again in Heaven. Aye ye who gave
    me birth!'

There was no possibility of turning back. They must continue on the route they had planned. Charlecote was occupied, and the preparations for the journey had been immense. Then, too, a return under such dread circumstances would only intensify the grief the stricken parents already felt. Mary Elizabeth continues her memoir by copying several extracts from her diary kept during this period.

12th November, 1840. We left Genoa and slept at Chiaveri, the road the whole way is very striking along the sea coast and the foot of the Apennines which are covered to the very summits with olives. We went on to Spezzia, the situation of which is quite enchanting, on the sea, and surrounded by vineyards and oranges and lemons with both fruit and blossoms, surpassing anything in beauty and size that I have ever seen. In the evening we walked on the shore of the treacherous waters that had drowned the poet Shelley, where we were accosted immediately by boatmen enquiring if we wanted boats. One in particular told us he had served the great English Milord who had died in Greece, the Milord Byron, but we would not trust ourselves to the tides of that dangerous bay.

November 25th. My birthday, a day always peculiarly sanctified to me and on which my mind used to love to dwell on the happy hours of my childhood when I knew no sorrow and but little sin. But now I am so full of sadness and can think only of my Herby and my Baby, both taken from me. But why, oh why should I so mourn when I know they have been saved all sin and sorrow, reclaimed as bright jewels in the Saviour's crown?

December 4th, Rome. We are here in the Palazzo Georgio in the Via Babuino, in a suite of apartments for which we are to pay 160 scudi a month. What scouring and cleaning we have had to do to make the rooms clean! A Russian countess with six pet dogs has been occupying them and every hole and corner is full of fleas.

Christmas Eve. Prince Doria sent us tickets for the Sistine Chapel, and George, Fulke, Mr Drake, Emily and I went at nine p.m. Ladies sat in boxes as at the opera. Between us and the Pope were strong iron bars, there were 12 old Cardinals seated on benches, dressed in scarlet robes, muttering their prayers to some very unheavenly music. It could not be called singing, it was more like the lowing of oxen. His Holiness is a very old and ugly man, arrayed in apparel glittering with gold and silver and a mitre sparkling with jewels.

Such ceremonies are paid to him that you might fancy you were in the presence of some pagan God. A Cardinal held his book, another turned over the leaves, a third took off his tiara, another put it on again, then a fifth held up some part of his robes and a sixth put on fresh ones. What all the ceremonies were for I know not, but they combined the grand with the ridiculous.

March 6th, 1841. In the evening Mr Lucy and I went to Princess Doria's which was a very fine assembly. Spent two hours most agreeably; had a very long *tête à tête* with the Prince who was very cordial, and was introduced to several people who promise to be pleasant. We are invited for every Monday evening till the Holy Week.

March 10th. Drove to the Pamphili gardens where I was enchanted with the wild flowers that perfectly enamelled the ground. We brought home such huge bunches of violets, the colour is far richer and deeper than the English violet but they do not smell half so sweet. Went in the evening to Prince Torlonia's. The Princess was a perfect blaze of diamonds, yet with all her riches I am told she is not happy; she had a prior attachment to a young man of noble birth, but without money, so her parents would not consent to the match and sacrificed her to the wealthy Torlonia who is nearly three times her age. I had a long chat with her; she is of the ancient house of Colonna. She is so lively and her eyes are so bright that I began to think old Torlonia after all cannot make her so unhappy.

Lord Byron's favourite, Countess Guiccioli, was there; she had a profusion of reddish auburn hair, and wears it in long ringlets, looking very much like a Titian Magdalene, though not half so beautiful. But time has laid its hand on her as on all others.

May 30th. We reached Naples yesterday and have a fine suite of apartments in the Hotel Croncelli. The dinners here are very good and the cook has the reputation of being the best in Naples. The view from our windows is too beautiful. The weather is humid and I would fain have slept alone to twist and turn in search of a cool spot for my burning feet, but my *caro sposo* will not hear of being without me.

June 1st. The month opened with the most glorious morning. I sat up in bed to watch the sun rising behind Mount Vesuvius with his golden mantle reflected in the calm and exquisitely blue water of the bay, and I thought of my dearest little Herby and my sweet tiny Edmund, gone to God, the great Creator of all.

June 10th. We were invited to a Ballo Reale, and George and I went. The ball room was most brilliantly lighted with hundreds of wax candles. The King and Queen with half a dozen brothers and sisters were seated on a bench covered with crimson silk. The King is a rather fine looking man, but very fat. He came and stood by me for about 10 minutes. The Queen is very short and very plain. They all danced and one of the Princes, without being introduced to me (they are privileged to ask who they like without an introduction), came up and asked me to dance, but I politely declined, which very much annoyed and astonished him.

I did not admire the Neapolitan ladies, they dressed without any taste, the belle of the ball was the present Duchess of Somerset. She is quite beautiful.

July 5. We got to Rome on the 30th and are established in the Palazzo Georgio again. The Prince and Princess Doria are kindness itself and through them we have become acquainted with all of the best families in Rome, from whom we receive endless invitations. The Shrewsburys too are here and we see a great deal of each other. I spend many mornings in the different artists' studios and delight in Gibson, Macdonald and charming old Thoralson who are always pleased to see us and show us their beautiful works. We have hired an Italian footman as Thomas is not much use excepting to valet George and Fulke and Spencer. We have an Italian coachman too and a Roman open carriage, and make excursions most days.

We undertook the tour in order to restore my health and raise our spirits, and to show our children the wonders of the Renaissance, but I confess that more often than not I had to hurry the girls past statues of naked gods that their native innocence might not be impaired; and as for myself, the blushes rose to my cheek when looking on Canova's recumbent marble figure of Pauline Borghese.

July 8th, 1841. Arrived at Venice. The hot weather withers all my bright ideas or I could say a good deal in praise of this wonderful city and lament the railroad which is fast making its way to spoil the city's beauty and the charm of its present approach by gondola. I should like to take a gondola back to Charlecote with my own gondolier to row me on the Avon. The Venetians never seem to go to bed if one may judge by the continual noise and chatter going on all night under one's window.

August 4th. Off at five o'clock in the morning to travel in the cool of the day as the heat is quite intolerable. Breakfasted at Padua and slept at Vicenza, then on to Lake Como where, sadly, the weather changed, with violent thunderstorms.

After dinner it cleared and we took a boat and rowed for two hours which delighted the children. Como's lofty banks are studded with villas and villages, and its waters are as deep blue as a sapphire.

At Lucerne it was again misty and rainy so we could not enjoy the lovely scenery. At Zurich we went on the lake but I was too unwell to enjoy it. I was very poorly and most anxious to get to Paris for my confinement.

On the 23rd August we arrived at Luneville and stayed there for the boys' sakes to see a review of cavalry by the Duc de Nemours who had reached Luneville with ourselves. On the 24th we arrived at Nancy meaning to leave the next day, but we know not what a day will bring forth, for the next morning, as the carriages were packed and the horses with the postilions cracking their whips, impatient to start, I was taken so very ill that the carriages were sent away and a doctor sent for, and at eleven o'clock that night my darling sixth son Edmund Berkeley was born. The circumstances of his birth, the perils past as they now rush upon my mind, seem like some romance.

The Hotel de France, which we were about to quit, was filled with officers, and the rooms we had occupied the night before were now to be occupied by the Duke of Nemours who was hourly expected for another grand review. However, duke or no duke I was rushed back into the room I had just left, followed by my husband, children and Hughes all in great alarm, and the gruff old landlady bidding us be off, she could not let us remain as every room in her hotel was engaged.

Desirée and dear Fulke went to try and get apartments elsewhere, but without success as every hole and corner in the town were filled for this expected review. A pretty hearing for me who was lying on the sofa in my travelling dress in a state of agony in mind and body, poor Spencer and Aymer sobbing bitterly, thinking I was dying, Hughes wringing her hands and crying, 'Oh! My dear, dear Mistress, what will become of us?' I sent for the landlady and told her I should appeal myself to the Duke, on which after much grumbling she consented to us remaining, but we must be content with the upper storey, so I had to crawl up a steep flight of stairs to a large comfortless bedroom with two small beds, one little table and three wooden chairs. There was a small room adjoining for my husband, and the children were stowed away somewhere. Thomas and Desirée had to find a bed where they could.

I had no baby clothes, as both clothes and an English monthly nurse were to meet me in Paris. Dear Emily and Carry set to work with their needles, and Hughes cutting up some of my linen and flannel, they soon made a suit for the expected baby. I shall not easily forget the hour of its birth. The doctor was in the next room talking French with my husband whilst Hughes kept crying out, 'Sir, do let Dr Simonion come to my dear mistress who is so very ill!'

When Baby was born he appeared to be dead, but Desirée, who had been waiting outside, was prepared in case of need with a warm bath, brought it instantly into my room and himself took the poor little thing and put it in, and presently it showed signs of life. So fortunate we had our own baths, for we should never have got one that night of revel amongst the officers, with no soul coming near to attend to us.

We stayed five long weeks at Nancy as my recovery was so slow. We received the greatest kindness from Dr Simonion and every one in the hotel, even from the cross old landlady who became so fond of us all that she was full of sorrow at parting with us.

On the 1st of October we arrived in Paris and took up our quarters at the Hotel Wagram in the Rue de Rivoli, where we had a very large and comfortable suite of apartments. It was just twelve months since our little Edmund died and I felt the whole weight of my sorrow once again, but I knew the precious child was at rest and I loved my little Nancian dearly.

After we got settled and had recovered from the enormous fatigue of the journey, we arranged with different masters to come and give lessons to the children: Fouché for dancing, Gillet for French, and Labarre for the harp. We hired a piano and a harp for me from Erard. Spencer went to a very good French day school and the girls studied with their father the masterpieces in the Louvre. We went to the opera several times and to the Theatre Française where we saw the actress Rachel in Racine's Phaedra. She was wonderful, acting with such reality that I lost my night's sleep, for I could not get her out of my head or from before my eyes. She can change her countenance and her voice in a manner perfectly startling.

We drove one day to Bagatelle, Lord Hertford's *maison de campagne*, the most perfect bachelor's house in the French taste I ever was in, and the grounds about it so splendidly laid out; but what a shame and pity it is that he should prefer it to his noble Warwickshire home, Ragley, which he utterly neglects. We saw also Lord Henry Seymour's stables full of such handsome riding horses. I longed to be on one of their backs and to be able to canter through the Bois de Boulogne where the leaves were taking on their autumn colours, instead of riding in a carriage as we were doing. In returning home we met Louis Philippe, as usual surrounded by numerous guards. His very carriage was made of iron in order to make his life more secure.

General de Rumigny, a personal friend of the King's, was most kind to us and took us over the private rooms as well as the State apartments of the Tuileries, the former are very plainly furnished, and he told me that the Queen and the Duchess of Orleans work for the poor of Paris, they are so good and charitable and devoted to the welfare of the French people; every evening they employ themselves in making clothes for them.

When we were in Italy we had received news that dear Brother had married Lady Sarah Amherst. Brother's views on matrimony had been expressed sometime earlier in a letter from which I now quote,

'The nearer women approach thirty, the more anxious are they to rule family and even husband himself, which makes me dread a wife too well experienced. Years of discretion are better not attained and ladies are best caught before they leave their teens, when traces of punishment and governess are not quite lost and forgotten.'

How seldom men act as they profess! Brother married a lady older than me, Lady Sarah being then 41. (She made him the best of wives and they were the happiest couple and had two daughters. She survived him fifteen years.)

Now, in Paris, I received a letter from dear Hugh to announce his intended marriage with Harriet Williams Wynne, Sir Watkin Williams Wynne's only daughter, and niece of the Duchess of Northumberland (with whom she had lived as her daughter since the death of her own mother, Lady Harriett Williams Wynne). It was an *enormous* match for him, a second son without fortune but what he could make by his own brains. However, her father and the Duke and Duchess, knowing his sterling worth, were satisfied and gave their full consent to the match.

The wedding was to be on the 16th of May so on the 10th we said goodbye to Paris. We started at five o'clock a.m. and got to London at 10 o'clock the next night. The following day was spent seeing relations and in the evening we went to the Stanleys to meet the Duchess of Northumberland, who spoke in the *highest* terms of dear Hugh and said she placed the happiness of her niece in his keeping with the *utmost* confidence.

The ceremony was quite regal, the bride was conveyed in the Duke's carriage, with four horses and outriders in all their state liveries, from Northumberland House to St Martin's Church and followed by half the coronet carriages in London. The Bishop of Carlisle performed the ceremony and after all was over the bride and bridegroom stepped into the Duke's carriage and were driven to Sion for their honeymoon. At two o'clock we adjourned to Northumberland House to partake of a splendid *déjeuner*, and in the evening we and all the relatives met at 21 Hill Street to rejoice over Hugh's good fortune.

At last, on the 20th of May 1842 our carriage rumbled under the Charlecote Gatehouse followed by the chaise out of which climbed Spencer and Aymer, their two sisters and the nurse carrying darling Berkeley who was scarcely ten months old. How great was our thankfulness at returning to the dear old place after nearly two years. Home, sweet home, there is no place half so dear to me, but my eyes did not remain dry when I thought of the deaths of two most dear and lovely boys, no longer here, and when I went into their nursery grief filled up the room of my absent children.

The Widow

In the autumn of 1844, dearest William Fulke went to Magdalen College, Cambridge, and on the 4th November my kind old mother-in-law died, having survived her husband nearly 21 years. Her death was most sudden, and deeply affected us all, but it was a blessed end, really like the extinction of a light which had burnt bright in its socket to the end. The evening previous to her death, I took her an apple (of which she was very fond) and she appeared in her usual health and spirits, and kissing me, said 'How good and kind you are, you dear darling, to think of me,' and she wished me good night. The next morning about five o'clock her maid rushed into her bedroom crying, 'Come, oh come! My dear mistress is dead! She called to me to give her some milk and before she put the cup to her lips she laid her dear head on my shoulder and was gone.' She was 86. As she lived so she died, at peace with God and man. She was buried in the Lucy vault in Charlecote church by the side of her husband, followed by her two sons George and John, her two grandsons, William Fulke and Henry Spencer and her two nephews, Newton and Leveson Lane.

The winter of 1844–45 was bitterly cold and the spring hardly better. The new wing where the family slept, in spite of fires in every room, was not warm. George's lassitude was alarming. No longer did he ride daily round the park in all weathers (when he did he had to be helped on and off his horse) but he seldom felt like braving the cold outdoors. The loss of his mother appeared to have deprived him of will to fight physical weakness. When there were guests staying in the house he hardly appeared. Increasingly concerned, his wife took him to London to consult Mr Johnson, Physician Extraordinary to the Queen. Back at home he seemed to fail rapidly.

Mr Johnson came down from London to see my dear husband on the 1st, 11th, 15th and 22nd of June, but instead of getting better he was getting rapidly worse and I was most wretched. I nursed him myself, night and day, he was too weak either to wash or dress himself. The doctor tried to persuade me to have a regular nurse as he said I should injure my own health, but I said that as long as God would give me strength nothing would induce me to give up attending to him, and I praise and bless God that I was able to do everything for him to the last. His sufferings were very great but he bore them without a murmur and with the utmost patience.

The first Sunday after Trinity was the last time that he was able to be at our evening family prayers, and hear the beautiful collect 'O God, the strength of all those who put their trust in thee.' Next morning Mr Johnson came again, and Mr Jephson and Mr England, to hold a consultation. Knowing he could not live they persuaded him to let them make his Will and brought it to me, saying, 'Mrs Lucy, you will have every reason to be satisfied with it, and he wishes to see you.'

I flew to his room with the Will in my hand and found him pale as death and trembling all over. Looking at me in the most agitated manner, he said, 'Mary, the doctors have been making my Will, I do not know what is in it, give it me,' and he broke the seal and desired me to read it to him. I cried, 'Oh, destroy it. I want nothing and if the younger children are to have such a sum dear Fulke can never live at Charlecote,' so he took it and tore it to pieces and told me to send for his man of business and he would make another, so I did, but when

Wallington arrived he was incapable. Hugh came and my poor husband was then able to tell him that he had destroyed the Will the Doctors had made and I showed him the pieces.

I never left his bedside from that moment. About ten o'clock p.m. he asked for all the children to be brought to him that he might bless them and take leave of them. Dear Aymer and the little Berkeley were got out of their cribs and came in their night clothes, and when we were all assembled weeping round his bed, he repeated again and again 'God bless you', and kissed us all, and then calling Spencer to come once more to him, he kissed and blessed and reblessed him (he was his favourite). The last words he spoke were, 'Into thy hands Lord I commend my Spirit,' and as the clock struck eleven that Monday night the 30th June 1845 he ceased to breathe. What words can express the anguish of my soul . . .?

George Lucy was in his fifty-sixth year. They had shared a life together for 23 years and now at 42 she was a widow with all the weight of the property and the children's futures on her shoulders.

My husband dying intestate I was sole guardian of my children, the eldest, dear Fulke, being still under age and the youngest only two years and ten months. I had many difficulties to contend with. My brother Hugh, looking into the affairs, said to me 'Mary, you must let Charlecote for you cannot possibly afford to live there and the pictures and valuable furniture must be sold to realise money for the younger children.' I said, 'No, I will not let or leave Charlecote even if I have to live upon a crust, nor shall any of the paintings or furniture be sold,' and, consulting dearest Fulke, he was of the same opinion and we agreed to have everything valued and for him to take the pictures, etc. at the price his father had given for them; and as happily that cruel succession duty had not been passed we were able to do as we pleased. I looked myself over all my husband's papers and a most painful and harrowing task it was.

★   ★   ★

The following July, Fulke returned from Cambridge. He had taken his degree with great credit and honours and, at the request of Lord Warwick, he accepted a captaincy in the Warwickshire regiment of militia. Being now of age, he desired that we should all live together till such time as he should marry, and we were all so united and bound together in love that we were only too happy to do so. I settled to give him £1000 a year and the children each made him a handsome allowance.

Mary Elizabeth felt it wrong to let her personal grief overshadow her children's lives. She modified her mourning in a way that would have been thought shocking a decade earlier and turned her full attention towards the needs and well-being of her children. All her life, family had been all the world to her. She had suffered the loss of parents, husband and two of her children. The others were fast growing up. Fulke was of age and, as her brother now reminded her, Emily must be launched. He wrote:

'How refreshing to find yourself in easy slippers, running from one flower bed to another. Still, London must be visited for Emy's sake; she must have a twirl in the swing of gaiety, although I expect it will devolve on some pleasant college friend of Fulke's to induce her to sigh under the shade of the old lime avenue. I hope dear Emy will find her head in a circle of rosebuds without any sharp points in the wires to prick her.'

It was almost prophetic: Emily's fate was coming towards her.

In the summer of 1847, we took a house in town between us, 19 Hanover Square, and Emily, Carry and I went up with the intention of remaining two months. Dear Fulke joined us soon after and our five riding horses from Charlecote came up all safe. We brought up the barouche and hired a coach for night work and wet days for six guineas a month and took a very handsome pair of brown carriage horses on approval.

Fulke and Emy rode together daily in the Park and did look so nice, and Carry and I often drove in the open carriage, made a round of calls, and ended with a drive round the Park, which was always so crowded with gay equipages that it was next to impossible to move along. But I was weary of seeing all the old and young faces of the *beau monde* that passed on like a magic lantern. My heart was heavy with memories of happy years now gone. These haunt me still, and my eyes grow dim with tears, but I look back to the past with great gratitude to the Almighty for innumerable blessings; yet there are days which seem harder than others.

Dear Fulke went to Lady Sefton's ball. As yet I had not gone to any, being still in mourning; consequently Emy had not, nor Carry, but cards came from the Duchess of Sutherland for her ball to meet the Queen and Prince Albert, so I consented for Emy's and Carry's sake. It was to be the ball of the Season and we went to Laville to order our dresses for it. When we returned that afternoon, Sir Robert Buxton called to offer to carry Emily to the Flower Show in Regent's Park, to which he knew we were going. But I proposed his taking Fulke which did *not* seem to please him; I should not of course have allowed one of my daughters alone with a young man.

Now for a description of the ball at Stratford House. Fulke, Emily and I arrived at ten o'clock and went up the grand staircase into the magnificent gallery a few minutes before the arrival of the royal party: the Queen, Prince Albert, the Grand Duke Constantine, the Duke of Saxe Weimar and several other foreign princes followed by the Duchess of Sutherland and her two lovely daughters, Lady Caroline and Lady Constance Leveson Gower. The Queen looked in *full pleasing* and bowed and smiled as she walked past us into the ball room, where she took her seat on a crimson velvet cushioned bench with the Duchess of Sutherland on her right hand and the Duchess of Saxe Weimar on her left; Prince Albert, the Royal

Princes, and the Duke of Wellington standing grouped around.

Presently the ball was opened by the Queen and the Duke of Saxe Weimar. She dances beautifully and is very graceful, though short and a bad figure. Her dress was white tarlatan embroidered in colours round double skirts, with a wreath of flowers mixed with many diamonds on her head, and in her hand she carried a bouquet nearly as large as herself.

The Duchess of Sutherland looked an empress in a dress of the richest white silk and fine lace trim'd with bunches of stephanotis and a profusion of diamonds on her head. All the gentlemen were in uniform or court dress and my dearest Fulke looked so handsome in his dress uniform worn for the first time. Dear Emily's dress was of white tulle, and in my eyes the prettiest dress there, and herself quite the pocket Venus.

Emily danced and enjoyed herself immensely and so did Fulke, and I enjoyed it too, seeing them so happy. We did not get home until four o'clock a.m.

The Queen was highly delighted and said she had come from her home to a palace, for the rooms were so magnificent, blazing with hundreds of wax lights, the flowers so rare and in such profusion, perfect showers of roses and garlands hanging from pillar to pillar in the grand entrance hall. There was a fountain in a recess in the ball room gushing into an immense white marble basin filled with white water-lilies.

Dear Emily was much admired and particularly by my old love Mr Wilson Patten, who had married five years after me his cousin, Anna Bold (now deceased) and had two sons and five daughters. He said to me, 'As you and I could not be man and wife, do let us hope that a marriage may take place between a son of mine and one of your daughters or vice versa, so that we may be united in our children.' I wish such a thing could have been but, alas, in a few years we both had great sorrow, for he lost his sons and two daughters and I mourned the loss of four sons and a daughter.

A few days after the ball, Spencer, Aymer and my precious little Berkeley came up and I drove to Euston Station to fetch them. What kissing! We all went to see the Bush People, the most horrible looking creatures from the interior of South Africa, little above the monkey tribe, wild and fierce, constantly chattering, growling and crouching; warming themselves by a charcoal fire. They roast and eat poisonous serpents and extract their bags of poison with which they cover the points of the arrows. There were two men, two women and a baby. One of the women was very anxious to get hold of Berkeley and tried her best to get him into her arms. He was so afraid of her and begged of me to take him home.

The next day I drove with the three dear boys to the zoological gardens in Regent's Park where they were so delighted I thought I should never get them away. We afterwards drove to Hyde Park and they said, 'Now Mamma, do show us the Queen!' and I had answered, 'How can I?' when Aymer cried, 'Here comes the Queen!' and true enough, there she was in a barouche like ours with four horses and outriders in their scarlet liveries. They were so pleased, and so was I to see them so.

That evening, Fulke, Emy, Carry and I went to a ball at Lady Palmer's where Emy first saw her future husband, Tom Fitzhugh. He was dancing with Carry when she said to me, 'Who is that handsome man? I must be introduced to him! Lucky Carry! How did she get to know him?' Before we left she *was* introduced to him and he danced with her. It was a very good ball, the rooms were spacious and beautifully decorated, the music so admirable. Prince Napoleon was dancing and thoroughly enjoying himself, I dare say little thinking he should one day be the Emperor of the French.

On the 17th we all left London and returned to dear Charlecote. How I did rejoice to be at the dear old place once more. Tom Fitzhugh and his sister came on the 23rd July, and on the 28th he proposed to my beloved Emily and was accepted and the next day, overflowing with joy, he left, soon to return.

The wedding took place on the 21st of October. The hall at Charlecote was filled with the guests and a large body of the tenantry. Dear Emily, in white silk, Brussels lace and orange flowers, soon made her appearance on Fulke's arm and attended by the bridegroom. Mr Wallington (being the oldest of the farmers) greeted her in the name of all her brother's tenants, clasped round her wrist a diamond bracelet as a token of their affection for her and for the love and respect they retained for the memory of her late father. It was a most touching and affecting sight, and one I can never forget.

We went in twelve carriages to the quaint little old church in the Park. The village bands of Charlecote, Hampton Lucy and Stratford united, drumming and fiddling away along the road as we passed, to the great danger of frightening the horses. A double arch of evergreens decorated with flowers waved over the Park gate and an archway of evergreens and flowers was erected from the churchyard gate to the church porch, which had a very pretty effect. The ceremony was performed by my brother-in-law, the Rev John Lucy, and as the lovely bride and bridegroom returned in their carriage their path was strewed with flowers by the village school girls.

About half past 12 o'clock, after changing her bridal dress for a travelling one of lilac shot silk and a bonnet of white terry velvet, my most dear Emily left the home of her childhood with her husband for Llandwyn, lent them by Sir Watkin Williams Wynne, for their honeymoon. We sat down in number 43 to a breakfast. Many speeches were made and healths drunk. Dearest Fulke made the most eloquent speech and won golden opinions from all present. At three o'clock every cottage on the estate was regaled with beef, plum pudding and good ale in the new loft over the stables which holds about 300. At nine o'clock the tenantry, their wives and sons and daughters began to arrive for a ball. They danced in the large dinner room and supper was laid in the Great Hall.

There was an excellent band and everything went off well and dancing was kept up with great spirit till four o'clock in the morning.

'Swift as shadow, short as any dream,' and all was over; my beloved Emily was gone. She carried away with her my very right hand, 'yea the very glow from our grate, the sun beams from our panes.'

Emily's wedding in the little church in the park renewed in Mary Elizabeth's mind a scheme which had been brewing ever since her arrival at Charlecote, when she had expressed her disappointment in the extreme shabbiness of the church in which 'not one architectural beauty remained'.

I had long wished to pull down the wretched old church in the Park and build a new one. Hugh tried to persuade me to do without an architect to save a fee but happily I bethought me of the old proverb 'penny wise, pound foolish', and made a choice of a Mr Gibson, a pupil of Sir Charles Barry's who had worked with him on the rebuilding of the new Houses of Parliament. He succeeded in giving me the utmost satisfaction, for he caught all my ideas and embodied them in the design, and was so kind, never thinking of any trouble I was giving him by altering this and that. He let me have my own way in every detail.

All the clergy in the neighbourhood were very importunate to be told my plans but I would neither show or tell them anything, not even John Lucy, as I did not ask for a farthing from anyone and did not want their opinions or advice. 'I would do what I pleased, and doing what I pleased I should have my will and having my will I should be contented; and when one is contented there is no more to be desired' (Don Quixote).

The last Sunday that divine service was performed in the old church I could not help feeling very sorrowful as it contained memories dear to my very soul. How many times since I had been a wife and a mother (now 26 years) with husband and children had I prayed in that old family pew with its large oak desk around which we had knelt together, then in the plain ancient Norman font all our children had been christened. Before that altar we had together received 'the bread of life', and the old church bell had rung its remorseless toll four different times and the burial service had been read for my beloved husband and three beloved sons, and once had rung merrily and the marriage service had been read for my dearest Emily. The recollection of these things kindled at my heart and caused my tears to fall fast on the old building as it fell to the ground and there was not one stone left upon another.

Her preoccupation with the rebuilding and the frequent consultations with the architect over the next two years were to become an almost God-given diversion when she sorely needed to be distracted from the further sorrow that was fast approaching.

In June 1848 the Willoughbys again kindly lent us their house in Hill Street and Carry and I went up, and Fulke was to join us in a week. His riding horses went up with ours but at the end of the week he wrote from Charlecote to tell me he had a bilious attack which would delay his coming up for a few days. However he grew worse and we all returned home and found him ill of the jaundice. And oh! with what a throbbing head and aching heart I even now think of that fatal illness—his patience, his goodness, his most perfect resignation, and I might say his willingness to quit this world.

Mr Hodgson from Birmingham attended him as well as Mr England and they both were sanguine as to his recovery, till it turned to black jaundice and then we lost all hope and he knew he must die. He made his will, leaving everything to his brother, Henry Spencer. Very early in the morning of the 28th he called me (for I had a little bed put up for me in his room that I might be always near him) and said he wished to receive the sacrament, so I fetched Mr Dayman. He then turned his loving eyes on me, saying, 'Dearest Mamma, I grieve to leave you but I am quite happy and content to die if it is God's will. I should like to have Aymer and Berkeley that I may kiss them, and please send for dear Emily Fitzhugh and my uncles and aunts that I may take leave of them all.' I rushed upstairs and in an agony of grief awoke dear Amy and Berkeley and brought them in their night clothes. He covered them in his kisses while they bathed him with their tears, sobbing their little hearts out for they doted on him and he on them. He soon after fell into a slumber which lasted till noon. When he awoke his first and last words were, 'Is dear Emily come?' He spoke no more, but again fell into a deep sleep. And when she arrived that night, O God! What grief! He was quite unconscious of her presence, and so he continued until he died at six o'clock on Saturday, July 1st, just three years and one day after the death of his father.

He was in his 23rd year and was cut down like a summer flower in its richest bloom, and all the bright anticipations of a long and happy life shrouded in the gloom of his early demise. His loss to me was quite irreparable for he was everything the fondest mother could desire: the most devoted son and the kindest of brothers. He was very handsome and had an elegant slim figure—he measured six feet. He was such a beautiful child that when in London his nurse was often stopped, and twice by royalty, to enquire his name. One fine day in June 1829 he was running by my side in Kensington Gardens when the Princess Victoria (now our gracious Queen) was tossing hay with a little rake, attended by her ladies, and he ran off towards her. When she saw him she exclaimed, 'What a lovely boy!', caught him up in her arms and kissed him.

I became so ill and broken hearted that I could neither eat or sleep or digest anything.

Spencer was by now turned eighteen and at a crammer's for the Oxford entrance. He came home at every opportunity and tried to fill the void the others had left. He was now the heir to Charlecote, his opinion was asked and taken on all decisions concerning the property. Very slowly Mary Elizabeth came out of the state of shock brought about by Fulke's death. Her brother Hugh Williams now had a house on the Compton Verney estate, which he managed for his brother-in-law, and rode over to Charlecote whenever he could, but he had a wife and, by now, children, and could not be at her side all the time. It was with thankfulness that they saw her begin to revive, once again taking an interest in the rebuilding of the little church which now housed so many members of her family.

The work on the new church absorbed me more and more, pushing back sorrowful thoughts from my mind as I watched my ideas daily taking shape. The dear children were to give a window in memory of their father. Thomas Willement, who had done so much for Charlecote's restoration twenty years earlier, asked to be allowed to design and present a rose window over the altar. Mr Gibson gave the window over the west door. The effigies of the three Sir Thomas Lucys had been wrapped in blankets and safely housed in a shed in the church yard until such time as they should be replaced in a Lucy chapel specially designed for them.

Spencer was now of age and showed himself a true son of his father by undertaking the restoration of the north wing. That part of the house had not been touched since the time of Queen Elizabeth and the walls were quite crumbling away. He made the additional improvement of throwing out oriels to the two wings of the house that fronted on the court. Mr Gibson, who had become a friend of us all, took the greatest interest and designed the much admired ceilings in the drawing and billiard rooms. Trollopes of Parliament Street, London, did the gilding and painting entirely after my taste and directions, with Spencer's approval. The amber coloured Chinese silk on the walls of the drawing room and the crimson Chinese silk curtains were bought many years before by my husband and for which he had given one guinea a yard. The oak was all off the estate and worked up by our own carpenter, by name Henry Kyte of Hampton Lucy, who had laid the floors in the large dinner room.

It was while the restoration was going on that a most alarming episode occurred. One morning I was awoken by a loud knock at my bedroom door, and on crying out, 'Who is there? What is the matter?' heard the deep voice of Foster the butler. 'It is me ma'am! Robbers have been in the house.'

'What have they taken?' cried I, starting up in bed.

'Everything,' he replied, 'but don't be frightened, ma'am'— when he had nearly frightened me out of my wits waking me out of a sound sleep with his tremendous rap tap at my door! Well, I sprang out of bed with my heart beating violently, thrust my arms into my habit body (it being the first article of dress which presented itself in my wardrobe), put on my slippers *sans* stockings or more clothing and flew downstairs to my sitting room. At the door stood Foster with his hair erect as though he had seen a ghost. I found the room in a state of confusion, the carpet strewed with work, worsteds, writing paper, pens, etc., and my writing desk, work box, cabinets, all broken open and their valuable contents gone. After casting a look of despair around, I went to the library where I found every cabinet, casket and drawer had been ransacked in a similar manner, and all the treasures and old family relics gone. The dinner and breakfast rooms had also been broken into, but fortunately there was nothing of value to steal. The drawing room, billiard room—and most happily, the plate room—had escaped their search.

After seeing with a hasty glance what valuables were missing, I turned to Foster and said, 'Now I must act and try to catch the thieves, and by and by I must wail and lament.' So I sat down, and with a hand shaking like an aspen leaf, I wrote a list of the stolen articles and despatched him off to Rugby (the then nearest telegraph office), sent off the grooms to make known the robbery at every station and neighbouring town, had bills printed with a description of the stolen goods and a

£100 reward offered for the capture of the burglars. All this was effected in a very few hours and the doleful news of the great robbery at Charlecote flew like wild fire over the neighbourhood, and the door bell had no rest from eager enquiries calling to learn if it were true.

On enquiry at Barford [*a village on the way to Warwick*] I found that two men, exactly answering a description of those seen by a workman employed on the church, had been at the two public houses on the Monday night and, seeing a little boy standing outside the door, had asked him whose great house that was on the road towards Stratford. The child replied, 'That great house was Charlecote, Mrs Lucy's.' Then, at Warwick, I ascertained that these same two men had arrived at the Crown Inn on the Monday morning, had asked many questions of the waiter respecting the principal houses in the neighbourhood, getting all the information they could from him. They then requested the landlord to take care of their two carpet bags whilst they went to see Warwick Castle.

Now I had clearly traced them from Warwick to Charlecote, but how was I to pursue them from Charlecote to the place of their destination with our stolen property? At Hatton I learned that two men had come to the public house there about six o'clock in the morning, had breakfasted on ham and eggs and left by the omnibus for Birmingham carrying with them two large carpet bags. Foster immediately went off to Birmingham and told all this to Glossop, the head of the police; and Glossop said, 'We shall have them, for I know who they are, notorious thieves! I know where they lodge—at 35 King Edward's Row. One is Evans, and brother to the woman who keeps the lodging. The other is a noted smelter in this town, by name Bradshaw.'

So to 35 King Edward's Row Glossop and a policeman Dutton went, but did not find either. All remained quiet, till about seven o'clock in the evening, when Bradshaw drove up in a cart. Glossop was prepared to seize him and as he was turning the corner of the street, Glossop threw himself upon him and knocked him down and, with the help of Dutton, captured him, but not before a violent struggle and an attempt to shoot Glossop with a revolver he contrived to draw out of his pocket, which had two barrels ready loaded. He had a carpet bag in his hand, a miniature of Sir Thomas Lucy 'of Shakesperian memory' and a purse containing 43£ in gold and a silver penny; also a pocket book in which were written entries of his travelling expenses to Charlecote; also notes referring to Warwick Castle, and the sums he had given there as 4s to the housekeeper, 2d for Great Tower, 1d to the porter at the gate, were found upon him.

Bradshaw and Evans were committed to stand their trial at Warwick at the Assizes and were lodged in Warwick gaol. Meanwhile, when Bradshaw arrived in custody at the Leamington station, he cried out to the people crowding round to get a look at him, 'Sixpence apiece for the sight of Jack Sheppard!'

Among the principal articles stolen were four very ancient and fine gold watches, the most valued and remarkable was one given by Charles II to Jane Lane. On its face was an exquisite small miniature of Charles set around with diamonds, the remainder of the face being beautifully painted with the sky and sun denoting the time by day and the moon and stars by night. There was also a very richly embossed (with figures) gold watch with splendid gold chatelaine and seals, and a very fine repeater which had belonged to the first Sir Thomas Lucy. Besides were many more rare and beautiful boxes, a number of beautiful seals with the Lucy crest and arms, a gold candlestick, some fine family miniatures, a gold medal of Shakespeare, quantities of valuable ancient coins and eight beautiful old purses. In one of these was all dear Berkeley's money with a silver penny.

On Tuesday the 6th May 1850 I was summoned to Warwick to attend the trial of the prisoners. Throughout the whole trial, which lasted several hours, Bradshaw kept his eyes constantly fixed on me, occasionally turning a most savage glance on

Fisher who had identified him. During his examination, Fisher could not resist saying to Bradsahw, 'How I wish I had seen you getting in through the glass door! Would I not have had a shot at you!' And Bradshaw boldly replied, 'I would have had a shot at you first, old fellow!'

Then last came my turn; the judge saying, 'Now let Mary Elizabeth Lucy be examined,' and I had to stand up and be sworn (a very awful proceeding) before the whole county of Warwick assembled in court; as well as the formidable judge himself and the many counsellors and lawyers with their eyes turned upon me, looking as grim and solemn as owls. I felt my tongue cleave to the roof of my mouth when I was called upon to answer the questions put to me. When the judge, with Bradshaw's purse full of money before him, said, 'Now Mrs Lucy, please to state the precise number of sovereigns and half sovereigns you lost,' I could not possibly do so as I was not like the King 'who sat in his chamber counting all his money'. I therefore replied that I believed the total sum to be between 40 and 50£. The money in the purse was then counted out and found to be all in sovereigns and half sovereigns to the amount of £54.10 and amongst them was a silver penny, which no sooner caught little Berkeley's eye than he called out, 'That is my silver penny!'

The judge then addressing the jury, asked them if they considered the money found on Bradshaw, with this silver penny, belonged to Mrs Lucy. The jury answered that this silver penny found with the gold on the prisoner was proof sufficient that it was Mrs Lucy's. The money was then handed over to me with the exception of £12 held back to defray the cost of Bradshaw's defence, which I thought was too bad, after being robbed, to have to pay the thief's counsel!

The judge then summed up the whole case and the prisoners were found guilty. Bradshaw was sentenced to 15 years' transportation and Evans 10. The lightness of the sentence surprised the prisoners as indeed it did all in court, and more particularly myself.

One of the officials at Warwick gaol came to Charlecote a few days later to beg I would see Bradshaw, for he had something which he wished to communicate. So I went, accompanied by my son Spencer. We were shown into the gaolers' private room, with my heart beating high with hope that the prisoner was on the point of discovering to me some of my lost treasures. In a few minutes Bradshaw appeared, and making me a low bow, began to make accusations against Glossop (the police chief) praying that I would not give him the £100 reward. He then expressed his regret that he had destroyed so many of my goodly things.

'Surely you have not destroyed King Charles's watch, and the other fine watches and the boxes of lapis lazuli in your smelting pot. You know better than that!' I exclaimed.

'Yes, I did,' he replied. 'I threw everything in for the sake of the gold. I wish I could now restore them to you. It always went to my heart to rob a lady.'

'I wish then,' cried I, 'that it had gone to your heart before you robbed me, even to my thimble.' I then exhorted him to turn from his evil ways, and to repent truly of his sins, and lead a new life. He seemed touched, bowed and withdrew; and so ended our interview. Then Evans came into the room and in the most sullen manner began to accuse the Birmingham police, and more particularly Glossop, as being the promoters and abetters of robbery and all crimes. I could get nothing from this red haired thief and had to return home with all my hopes crushed, with the knowledge that my treasures and much valued old family relics were irretrievably lost in Bradshaw's smelting pot.

Bradshaw returned with a ticket of leave in 1859. The Rector of Bradshaw's parish told me he had seen him and that he was anxious to come to Charlecote and have an interview with me, but I was afraid of seeing such a desperate rogue, so wrote and asked him to communicate by letter anything he wished to say and I mentioned that Evans had written about the watch etc.

being hid under a railway bridge and that he must restore it to me on his return to England. The following is his answer.

Birmingham, September 24 1857. Madam Lucy. In reply to yours of the 22nd I am sorry to say I cannot accede to your request as you allude to certain points I cannot solve by letter under any circumstances whatever. I, therefore, condole with you upon the loss of such property, and were it in my power to throw any light on the subject I would gladly do so, but I have settled down in life to serve God and Man in an honest way as God doth give me strength. Neither do I associate with my former bravadoes. I am, dear madam, yours respectfully, John Bradshaw.

Thus ended my correspondence with these notorious and hypocritical villains.

1850–1857

Victorian Summer

And now I must write an account of Carry's first Drawing Room, which took place on Thursday the 20th June 1850, and of the Queen's kindness to us.

When we got into the first room at the head of the stairs at St James's Palace, the crowd and crush of ladies fat and lean was so great that it was simply impossible to make one's way through the door. I did all I could to protect poor Carry, but was almost squeezed to death myself, and when at last we did get into the large room or gallery next to the throne room, Carry fainted away. Lord Gough, dear old man, took her up into his arms and carried her to the open window. Many ladies offered their smelling bottles and the Palace officials got sal volatile and water, but she was so very long before she came to herself that Lady Stanley of Alderly, passing through to go away, said to me, 'If you don't get your daughter into the Throne Room directly, the presentations will be all over and then you know you will not get to the Queen's ball.'

Poor Carry soon after this recovered and we entered the Throne Room at one door just as the Queen went out at the opposite one, which was too distracting. A lord-in-waiting, who was our great friend, and saw how unfortunate we had been, went at once to the Lord Chamberlain and introduced us to him and we told him our misfortune. He promised to make our disappointment known to Her Majesty.

Carry and I dined with Lady Trollope after the drawing room and everybody was full of our misfortune, and condoling us and saying, 'What a pity! How unlucky! Poor Carry, to miss this ball, for the Queen will not have another Drawing Room this season,' etc. But the next day a friend called and brought us the kindest enquiries after Carry from the Queen, hoping she was quite recovered, and saying that she should consider her as having been presented—that the name of Lucy was well known to her, and that very afternoon we received a card of invitation for her ball on the 9th of July.

Oddly enough, on the night of the ball we were nearly too late once again: Brown (the coachman) was so anxious that we should arrive in good time that, instead of falling into the line of carriages as ordered, he boldly drove down Constitution Hill to the private entrance to Buckingham Palace. I put down the window and called out, 'Brown, you are going quite wrong, and we shall be sent away,' but he heeded me not and when we arrived at the Palace, the Queen's footman asked me if we had the entrée and I was obliged to say no, but I was vexed and sorry that my coachman had made a mistake in bringing us there. He then said to Brown, 'Turn your carriage round, go back and join the line.' 'Oh!' I exclaimed, 'Do not send us away, it is my daughter's first ball and if we are now turned back we shall not get to the ball till morning.' So he had pity on us and bid us be quick and follow him for Her Majesty would arrive very soon. So out of the carriage we jumped, and only just in time, for the Queen came almost immediately and we stood on one side for her to pass, she giving us a most gracious smile.

It was at that ball that a Warwickshire neighbour, Mr Sheldon, who was with Mrs Sheldon, walked straight up to me and said, 'Mrs Lucy I want to ask you a question and beg you will answer it truthfully.' I wondered what it could be but said I would if I could. Then he said, 'I have been looking at you for the last half hour and cannot see a single grey hair in your head. Now what do you use?'

'Nothing,' I answered.

'Oh! No, no, that will not do. I am much your junior and yet am getting very grey. Now be truthful, for you know you are no chicken!'

'Well,' I replied, 'the old hen does nothing and her feathers are as God made them,' and I walked to the other end of the room, saying to myself, 'What a rude bear, he must have had too much champagne.'

On the 3rd July, Spencer went with Berkeley and me to see the Crystal Palace Exhibition. It was opened on the 1st May and great fears were entertained in many quarters that the bringing together of such an immense crowd, as might be expected on the opening day, would be made the occasion for some popular outbreak. The Queen understood the temper and the loyalty of her people too well to have any such fears. How right she was was fully proved by the universal good humour and enthusiasm that everywhere prevailed on that day.

Spencer, Berkeley and I were enchanted, delighted and bewildered with excitement as we entered the great hall of Sir Joseph Paxton's building. One general effect of beauty had been produced by the infinitely varied work of the thousands who had separately co-operated towards this marvellous display, and the structure in which it was set, by its graceful lines and the free play of light which it admitted, seemed to fulfil every condition that could be desired for the setting of the treasures thus brought together.

This glorious Crystal Palace was closed on the 15th October, 1851, a very wet day, appropriate to the really mournful ceremony of the closing of this great exhibition. The total sum received from all sources was £500,000 and the number of visitors to the building ran up to 6,200,000! And not an accident.

Revived at such a distance in time, memories are bound to have lacunae and recourse had to be made to diaries for local occasions, visits, health and weather. But since the purpose of the journals was to make instructive and amusing reading for the granddaughters, some episodes were omitted. It follows that a cause célèbre that upset the even tenor of life at Charlecote in March of 1852 is not mentioned by Mary Elizabeth. It involved poor Carry and gave her a reputation for being rather 'fast', though there is no evidence that she was anything but what the Victorians called 'a little bit giddy'.

She was walking home to Charlecote one day when she was overtaken by members of the hunt, riding home after a short day's hunting. One of these, Colonel Shirley of Ettington, asked her if she often walked alone to which she replied, 'Generally.' He then put up his horse at a farm they were passing and said he would walk back with her to Charlecote. She declared later that their conversation was of a lively (probably flirtatious) character but that 'there was nothing in it that all the world might not have been witness to'.

The lane was muddy and to avoid dirtying her shoes she climbed on to a strip of grass verge, he following. A labourer, one William Gimes, setting beans in an adjacent field, happened to look over the hedge and saw, or said he saw, Miss Lucy lying on the ground with her petticoats round her waist. He said he saw her drawers; the lady did not appear to be struggling. According to Carry, Colonel Shirley attempted to 'salute' her, whereupon she had had a hysterical fit and collapsed on the ground. The gentleman apologised vehemently. Her words to him were, 'You have not only insulted me but mischief will be made of it.'

He tried to pacify her and prevent her from rushing home, sobbing, to her formidable mother, but she was so agitated that nothing he could say would calm her. In the legal enquiry into the affair, officiously set going by Caroline's uncles, John Lucy and Hugh Williams, much was made of her temporary unconsciousness. She had no recall of what had actually happened. The jury of county neighbours were satisfied that Gimes's statement had been made in the hope of getting hush-money from the Lucys and the case was dismissed. Gimes lost his job and Carry was taken on a visit to Wales in order to recover her spirits and allow the episode to blow over.

In October, Spencer, Carry and I went to Llanover to Sir Benjamin and Lady Hall for the Eisteddfod at Abergavenny. We had a very long and wearisome journey and arrived so late that dinner was over, and though we were expected, nothing had been ordered in the shape of food for us, and we were dying of hunger. A footman showed us to our bed rooms and left us. I said to Tizzard, 'Do go down and bring us something to eat.' We waited a considerable time before she returned. She declared she had the greatest difficulty in getting anything, and what she did bring us was only enough for one, a cold slice of beef or mutton and some bread, which we three soon ate. Carry was so tired she went to bed but I dressed as quickly as I could and went down stairs with Spencer where Sir Benjamin and Lady Hall greeted us very warmly and introduced us to their guests, a most formidable proceeding for they were legion. Among them were the Count Esterhazy, the Duke of Somerset and his lovely daughter Lady Ulrica Somerset, Lady Langdale and her daughter Miss Bickensteth (an heiress), Sir John and Lady Shelley and their daughter, an heiress also.

When I went up to bed I noticed a piece of paper pinned on my pincushion with this written on it, 'A fly ordered to take you to the Eisteddfod each day during the week and the charge one guinea a day.' I thought to myself, this is a queer place, and so it seemed was the general opinion, and some wag wrote on their entrance gate, 'A park without deer, a house without cheer, a cellar without beer; Sir Benjamin Hall lives here.'

The next day just as Carry and I were putting on our things to go to Abergavenny there was a knock at the door and Lady Hall's maid entered carrying two frightful linstey petticoats and bodies, two Welsh chimney-pot black hats with coarse mob caps and said, 'If you please, her Ladyship wishes you and Miss Lucy to wear these Welsh costumes today at the Eisteddford,' laid the things down and, before I could give an answer for laughing, she went off.

Tizzard exclaimed, 'Oh! Ma'am you will surely never put on such ugly things and take off your own beautiful dress and pretty new bonnet! And Miss Lucy, Oh! She must not make herself such a guy.'

'No, no,' I cried, 'we will not.' But Carry (who never thought of herself) said, 'Oh! Never mind, Mamma, we had better do as Lady Hall wishes and perhaps all the other ladies will be dressed in these costumes.'

I replied, 'Tizzard, go and ask,' so she did and came back saying all the ladies were furious but were putting on the Welsh dress etc. which Lady Hall had sent to each of them. So Carry and I took off our pretty dresses and put on the frights. The hat was much too large for me and was so heavy it did nothing but come down half over my nose, and the linstey so hot, I never was more uncomfortable, and vowed I would never wear such horrible things again to please any Lady Hall, nor did I, and all the other ladies agreed with me and we returned our linsteys and hats etc. to her Ladyship that same evening and made her very angry.

The following morning when we ladies were sitting in the drawing room, some with work, some with a book and some doing nothing, Spencer rushed into the room saying, 'Make haste Mamma, put on your bonnet and come with me to a house in the park and hear a young man play the harp who will drive you wild.' So I flew upstairs, popped on my bonnet and went with him to the house, not far off, where Mrs Waddington, Lady Hall's mother, lived and died, and which was now filled with guests invited for the Eisteddfod, who had not handles to their names.

When we got there, Mr Thomas (for he was the young man) was just going away and had put the cover on his harp. Spencer said to him, 'Oh! I am so sorry you have done for I brought Mamma to hear you play.' On which he most good-naturedly uncovered his harp and played *La Danse des Fées*. I was enchanted and fancied the king of the fairies himself swept the cords, never did I hear such feeling, tone, richness and power combined. He told us he was staying at Llanover and was appointed 'Judge of Music' at the Eisteddfod to award the prizes to the best harpists; and at the last meeting, when he was a little boy of eight years old, he had won the best prize with a Welsh harp.

On the first day of the meeting the Rev David James had made a speech in which he gave a short sketch of Mr Thomas's career, I little thinking that it was the same young man who was 'to drive me wild'! He said that some years ago a youth had come into this hall to compete for the best prize for the harp and was successful. Through the influence of the Countess of Lovelace admission was gained for him into the Royal Academy of Music where he remained six years and then, outstripping every competitor, obtained the appointment of Professor of the Harp at that institution and the appointment of the first Harpist at her Majesty's Theatre. After retaining these for six years he went abroad in order to become known to the distinguished musicians in the great capitals of Europe.

When I found Mr Thomas was actually in the same house with us I asked Lady Hall why she did not let us hear him sometimes, for his playing was simply glorious, and I added he seems so nice and gentlemanlike; but the provoking and tyrannical woman said, 'No, you would spoil him, he must keep in his room and study.' Every evening the party from Mrs Waddington's joined the grander party in the big house and adjourned to the Hall, and the servants were sent for to dance Welsh gigues and wonderful capers.

One night there was a subscription ball at Abergavenny to which we all went, and Mr Thomas too, but Lady Hall disapproved of his dancing which we all thought was really too bad for all the young ladies would have been delighted to have had him for a partner. As I did not dance he sat with me most of the evening and I found him full of information and so agreeable that I was charmed with him, though I little thought from that time we were going to be life-long friends.

When the Eisteddfod was over, Sir Benjamin never offered to give the gentlemen any shooting, which Sir Harry Vane and Spencer were longing for, but planned a drive or a ride, marshalling everyone as to how they were to go, perfectly regardless of their own wishes. He generally desired me to sit beside him in a dog cart, a place of honour no doubt, but far from agreeable.

Sir Benjamin and his lady were anything but a genial host and hostess. One morning we happened to be a large party together in the drawing room where Sir Harry Vane and Spencer were very merry and making us all laugh (her ladyship was not present), when the door opened and Sir Benjamin, looking extremely grave, and the Duke of Somerset as stiff as a poker, walked in and said, 'I beg you will not all laugh so loud as I do not like noise,' and before we could recover from our astonishment and make any reply, he vanished and His Grace along with him.

He did not allow smoking, but the Count and Spencer smoked in their bed rooms and were often joined by Lord Bateman and Sir John Shelley till they were found out and then there was a terrible row. Lord Bateman was very good looking and full of fun, he told me he had come to Llanover with the intention of making up to the heiress Miss Bickersteth but on seeing her he no longer desired to make her his other half. She had made up her mind to be the Countess Esterhazy and as the saying is 'set her cap' at him, but alas! In vain. He found out her little game and said to Lord Bateman (who laughing told me) that however rich she might be he could never admit a pill into his hundred quarterings, alluding to her father who began life as a doctor and, so curious, had brought his future wife, who was Lady Oxford's daughter, into the world. He then left the medical profession and took to the law, where his great abilities soon caused him to rise. He became Master of the Rolls and from plain Mr Bickersteth was made Lord Langdale and married the Lady Elisabeth Harley.

Spencer was desperately smitten with the lovely Lady Ulrica and I think it was mutual.

Mrs Herbert, Sir Benjamin and Lady Hall's only daughter, gave a ball to which all the Llanover party were invited, and she specially named Mr Thomas. The two houses were only about five miles apart. Soon after we entered the ball room Miss Bickersteth who, notwithstanding her designs on Count Esterhazy, had really lost her heart to Mr Thomas, asked him to dance which he modestly declined, saying that perhaps it might annoy Lady Hall. But Miss Bickersteth would take no denial, and Lady Shelley said, 'Nonsense, Mr Thomas, you cannot refuse a lady when she asks you to be her partner,' so he stood up and they danced together. Lady Hall, seeing them, flew at him like a tigress and insisted on his retiring. Then we all attacked her and defended Mr Thomas, Mrs Herbert too came to the rescue and remonstrated with her mother and there was quite a scene. But Mr Thomas was triumphant and danced and enjoyed himself for the rest of the evening, the young ladies vying with each other who should secure him for her partner.

Mr Thomas came to Charlecote soon after our return and I gave a music party to which my neighbours to the number of 30 came. Everyone was in raptures with his playing. Lady Louisa Percy said she had never liked the harp till she heard Mr Thomas who had simply enchanted her! On the 23rd he was obliged to go but promised to return in about three weeks.

I had a great many lessons on the harp from Mr Thomas and during the first lesson Spencer and dear Aymer happened to be in the room when Mr Thomas said, after I had played a simple air, frightened out of my wits, 'Mrs Lucy, you bring such a fine tone, I am delighted, but I am sorry to tell you that you hold your hand badly with your thumb down instead of up. You must unlearn what you have been taught and I will make you a really fine player.'

Spencer and Aymer cried out, 'Oh! Mr Thomas, you must not make Mamma unlearn what she now knows. We like her playing and she is old and before she has learnt your way it will be time for her to die.'

They did make me laugh, and turning to Mr Thomas I said,

'If you can make me a fine player I will try and hold my thumb up and do whatever you bid me.'

Mr Thomas kept me to scales and exercises for the first year, and I did learn his way, and before I was *very* much older was able to play many a difficult duet with him. I would get up an hour earlier to have a good practice before breakfast, and I used to go to sleep trying to hold my thumb up.

In September, Carry and I had a charming expedition to Eywood to visit Lord and Lady Langdale for a fortnight, and Mr Thomas was invited also. A large party assembled, amongst the guests some Poles and Hungarians, a Count Teleki and a Monsieur Remery (a very clever violinist). Lady Langdale was so hospitable and kind and always finding out something pleasant for every day, and for every evening, and it was quite Liberty Hall, each one doing as they liked best. There were carriages and horses for you to drive or ride, there were picnics, a flower show, long walks, flirtations, dancing and music, and two harps upon which Mr Thomas and I played duets.

One afternoon we all went for a long walk, and going through a meadow there was a ditch which we jumped over, except Miss Bickersteth who declared she could not possibly jump it, when Count Teleki—more gallant than even Sir Walter Raleigh of old—lay down and, stretching himself full length across the ditch, bid Miss Bickersteth make a bridge of him, which she did and stepped over his back and we all screamed with laughing. I told Lady Langdale I felt sure the Count had an eye for her daughter, but she said, 'Oh! No, you are mistaken, he would not presume to think of such a thing, he is only a poor exile and his whole heart and mind are given to his unhappy country, but we are very fond of him, and he is teaching us Hungarian.'

I thought to myself, you blind mother, your eyes will be opened when it is too late, and so it came to pass for as soon as her daughter came of age she married him, and the wicked Count (for he *was* wicked) when he found that her fortune was strictly settled so that he could not spend it, he wished her goodbye three days after her wedding, saying he had a wife and a large family in Hungary. She never saw him again, and died a miserable woman not many years afterwards.

But to go back to Eywood; one evening after dinner we all adjourned to the grand staircase to hear Monsieur Remery play his violin. He was to stand on the top of the stairs and the effect, Lady Langdale said, would be startling, and indeed so it was. I shall not easily forget the wild wizard-like music, the wailing, then the piercing tone he drew from the strings. Then the foreigners proposed playing at different games to show off their agility, so chairs were brought and placed back to back, and they were to jump over them. After they had done this, Mr Thomas and other gentlemen said they could do the same, and so they all tried and jumped over the chairs quite as cleverly; then Count Teleki and a Polish baron (whose name I forget) challenged them to balance themselves on the upstairs rail of the staircase, which we ladies protested against as it was so dangerous. However, they would do it. Mr Thomas declared it was not difficult and he could do it, but in balancing himself he overbalanced, and as I was standing with Lady Langdale just underneath, down he came on my head and knocked me down flat on my knees, most fortunately for him as had he fallen on the marble floor in all probability he would have been killed; as it was he was happily saved all injury, and poor me only bruised my knees black and blue! Everybody was very much frightened and wished to help Mr Thomas and me up again, but when they found we were not seriously hurt they all laughed so loud and so long that the hall rang again with their peals of excitement at this most extraordinary and ludicrous termination to the games. However, after this no one felt inclined to balance on the staircase any more, and I limped up to bed, thankful that it was not worse.

In 1853 the new church was finally finished and the Fitzhughs, Mr Gibson and the Bishop of Worcester came to Charlecote for the opening of it, which took place on dear Emily's birthday, the 2nd of February. The weather was perfect and the congregation not only filled the church but the church yard. I could get no seat and was obliged to stand in the nave for the most part of the service, but on that day and in that hour I little heeded where I stood as long as I could pour out my heart in thankfulness and gratitude to God within the walls of that little church He had permitted me to raise to His honour.

Among the beautiful and simple-hearted customs of rural life in some parts of Wales, are those of strewing flowers before the funerals and planting them on the graves of departed friends. These it is said are the remains of some of the rites of the primitive church, and that once the custom of decorating graves was universally prevalent. Now the new church was finished, I tried to revive the beautiful custom of roses and lilies blooming over the dead, and doing away with those frightful tomb stones recording the names and virtues of the departed in large white or black letters. I met with opposition from a few whose ugly upright tomb stones still disfigure the church yard, but most were pleased to let me remove them and substitute them for stone crosses or lay them down even with the turf.

In some parts of North Wales the peasantry kneel and pray over the graves of their deceased friends for several Sundays after their interment; and where the tender rite of strewing flowers is still practised, it is always renewed on Easter, Whitsuntide and other festivals.

When I think of these things, I long for the remains of all those dear ones, now resting in the mausoleum, to be instead under the soft green turf that I might plant roses and lilies on them and water them with my tears and tend them with my own hand, and be buried by them knowing that my dear children would plant a rose or sweet violets over me, and sometimes water them with their tears. 'The grave, oh the grave, buries every error, covers every defect, extinguishes every resentment! From its peaceful bosom spring none but fond regrets, and tender recollections.'

In November [1854] my darling Aymer came home from Oxford very unwell. He had had rheumatic fever when at Christ Church in the spring but we hoped he had quite recovered and, after being in Scotland, appeared in excellent health. But the confinement and study at college made him ill again and obliged him to leave. I consulted Dr Evans, a very clever man from Birmingham and, to my inexpressible grief, he thought that Aymer's heart was affected—he had a blister on it.

Dr Evans came again on the 19th and dearest Aymer had to keep to his bed. On the 23rd Evans saw him again, and he got better. On Christmas Day he went to the new Charlecote church and received the Holy Sacrament, and afterwards he walked with us to the village to see some of the old people to whom he had given beef for their Christmas dinner. It was another very cold day and, alas, the next morning he awoke with a sore throat and became seriously ill, but still did not keep his bed, and only for some time his room.

On the 28th January at his own request, we had a bed put up at the foot of mine in my bed room (that room in which he was born, as well as his three dear brothers, William Fulke, Herbert and Davenport, and in which his dear father had breathed his last—and which I called 'the fatal room' as all who first saw the light there had died). And then oh! The anguish of my soul! I felt—I knew—he would not long be in this world. Oh how I prayed by him! How I wept by him! How I watched and nursed him and oh! how I cried unto God to bless those means used for his recovery, and restore him to health.

On Sunday 8th February, his last Sunday, Carry and I read the whole of the church service to him and the Rev Herbert Peel administered the Holy Sacrament to him and us. On Tuesday evening he evidently thought his end was near and did not like us to move from him as he lay on the sofa, or rested in the arm chair in Carry's room (the dressing room through mine). She had a piano on which I played all his favourite airs—for he was very fond of music—then read, then prayed by him.

The moon that evening was more than usually bright, shining into the room, and I observed him looking long and wistfully at it (for he would not have the blind drawn down) till he fell asleep and slept for about an hour in the easy chair. When he awoke and found it was eleven o'clock he was grieved that I had not gone to bed. We then put him in his bed but he soon became very restless and could not lie down for he could not get his breath, so I prop'd him up with pillows and I knelt down beside him and prayed, he praying with me and endeavouring to follow my words. And so he continued for about two hours, in much suffering, but perfectly sensible, calm, and patient and resigned.

When I saw his dear face was chilled with the damp dews of life's last struggle, my sobs (which I vainly strove to stifle) awoke poor Carry in the next room and she rushed, in an agony of grief, to her dearest Amy on whom she had so long waited with the most unwearied devotion throughout all his long illness. She took his hand in hers and bathed it with her tears and kisses. He could not speak; but never, oh never can I forget that last keen look of farewell. All was hushed as his guileless soul passed from earth to heaven and his spirit seemed to say, 'Weep not for the day that lies here, the shackles are broken; what earth could not hold nor love longer detain can neither be fettered by death.'

The clock struck two a.m. as he expired on the 11th of February in the twenty-first year of his age. I cried 'O God of all mercy support us under this burthen of misery. Oh! My son, my beloved Aymer, how shall I live without thee!'

On Wednesday the 18th February his loved remains were borne along that same old avenue of elm to the new church of Charlecote where in the new mausoleum he was laid between his dear brothers William Fulke and Herbert Almeric—his two only surviving brothers, Spencer and Berkeley, with his uncles John Lucy and Hugh Williams, following him, weeping, to his last resting place. That day an unspeakable anguish and yearning at my heart impel'd me to enter that vaulted chamber of death and once more stand by the remains of those so dear. I did stand there alone and hold sympathetic commune with their beloved spirits. I trembled, I prayed, yes, I did pray with all my soul, with all my strength, that it might be God's will to spare all the dear children still left me, and bless them with health and long life, and take me first.

1859–1864

Carry

In May (1859), although we took a house in London, 19
Bruton Street, I had no heart to enter into any gaieties. We had
our riding horses and I rode daily with Carry or Spencer, as the
exercise was absolutely necessary for my health. I took up my
harp and had more lessons from Mr Thomas and when my
own sad thoughts I could not shun, I touched its strings and it
seemed to light up a flame of cheerfulness in my mind, and
with some mysterious sympathy to gather tidings from
another sphere.

Spencer acted chaperone to Carry, and one day they dined
with the Stuart·Lanes and there she met Captain Pawlett Lane.
He called the following day in Bruton Street. I was out riding
with her and as we were returning through Berkeley Square he
was standing at the corner of Bruton Street, evidently waiting
for us, and Carry then introduced him to me, but I did not see
much of him. I returned home on the 15th July and Carry went
on a visit to Mrs Lane at Brighton, and on the 21st I went to
Brighton at her invitation and to my dismay found Captain
Pawlett Lane there as Carry's lover. Shortly after my arrival
they both implored my consent to their union, but I was
miserable and a terrible scene ensued. I knew nothing of his
character or family, and moreover he was such a very big
man—six foot two inches at least—and she such a little delicate
creature.

That night I was called up (I did not sleep at Mrs Lane's as her house was full, but I had rooms not far off) to come immediately as Carry was taken very ill. In an agony of fright I jumped out of bed and, hardly giving myself time to dress, ran as fast as I could to Mrs Lane's and found poor Carry in a fainting state, but I soon brought her to herself. The excitement of the previous evening had been too much for her. The following day the Stuart Lanes in vain assured me that Pawlett was everything that my fond heart could desire as a husband for my dear child, that he was the eldest son of Mr Lane of Badgemoor, a charming place in Oxfordshire—a very good old family, though no relation to them—and that he would have £2,000 a year. However, nothing could reconcile me to the match as I found that his regiment was ordered out to India shortly, and that Carry was determined to accompany him.

After we left Brighton we stayed a day in London where Pawlett's father met us. He behaved most honourably for he told me plainly that he should indeed be proud to be allied to the Lucys but he considered it his duty to inform me that his son had debts and no income beyond his pay as a captain, therefore no fortune to keep a wife. Eventually he would have Badgemoor, but he could not promise £2,000 a year.

Carry declared her fortune (which was about £14,000) would be enough and that she was willing to make any sacrifice in order to become Pawlett's wife. Man and wife! Ah me! for the greatness and the littleness of the bonds these names stand for!

On the 25th we got back to Charlecote where Spencer had already arrived. Pawlett followed us to ask Spencer's consent, which, after much pressure, he most unwillingly gave and persuaded me to do likewise. Carry being of age could of course marry *without* our consent but she loved us too dearly to give herself away without our sanction.

The wedding took place on Wednesday the 2nd September at Charlecote. At about half past ten o'clock the guests and tenants assembled in the Great Hall when the bride entered on

Spencer's arm, attired in white silk with two deep flounces of Brussels lace (my gift), a wreath of orange flowers and myrtle round her pretty fair hair and over it a very beautiful Brussels lace veil (the gift of her Aunts Harriet and Emma Williams). Old Mr Wallington, in the name of all the tenants, presented her with a splendid bracelet, a serpent of diamonds and blue enamel, as a token of their esteem and affection, and the good old man clasped it round her wrist as he had done 10 years since on a similar occasion to her sister Emily Fitzhugh. She received numerous presents; one not so costly—but quite as valuable in her eyes, being the offering of sincere love from the poor old men and women, young men and children of the villages of Charlecote and Hampton Lucy—a locket, chaste and simple, but very handsome. The Charlecote servants gave her a chain of pure gold to be attached to the locket, and which she put round her neck on the auspicious morn.

Six short weeks after their marriage, Pawlett and poor Carry had the sore trial of parting. Pawlett was obliged to join his regiment in India at the beginning of that fearful mutiny and war but only six months later dear Carry had the happiness of having him back from India in perfect health and without a wound. He had been promoted to the rank of Major. He kindly brought me five pearls, they were part of the loot taken at Lucknow. I have had them set in two rings.

On the 10th of July 1860, I was just stepping into the carriage to go to an afternoon 'At Home' with Miss Burdett Coutts when I got a telegram from Pawlett dated Tongswood in Kent (a place he had rented) asking me to come immediately as dear Carry was taken ill. (She was expecting her confinement shortly and I was to be with her.) Oh what an agony of mind that telegram put me in. I changed my dress as quickly as possible, and, with Tizzard and necessary luggage, I started off by train. When I reached Tongswood station the station master met me and said Major Lane had ordered a fly to be in readiness for me. His carriage had already been to meet the early train expecting me by that, and it had taken two London doctors who had been telegraphed for, as Mrs Lane was very ill. No words can describe my feelings of anxious terror.

When I arrived at the gate leading to the house I saw poor Pawlett pacing up and down like one distracted. I jumped out of the fly and cried out, 'Oh! Is she alive?'

'Yes, but so ill! Oh, so ill! She does nothing but call for you.'

In a moment I was at the bed side. She was overjoyed when she saw me, and kissing me said, 'My own darling Mamma, now you are here I shall be better.'

The two doctors were holding a consultation whether it would be possible to do without instruments—Pawlett exclaiming, 'Save my wife, Oh! Save my wife!' It was really heart-rending to hear him.

The doctors, as it was getting on for eight o'clock, wished for some dinner and went down stairs, and I remained with dearest Carry who was so patient and even cheerful as she was so happy to hold my hand in hers. When the doctors returned they had decided that instruments must be used. They requested me to leave the room, which I did not, but knelt down concealed behind a curtain and prayed to the Almighty to spare the life of my beloved Carry, and doubtless my prayers were heard. God be praised! At 10.15 p.m. my first grandchild was born. A fine boy and his dear mother, considering, wonderfully well.

I took him and washed, dressed and fed him, as the monthly nurse was too much engaged with my dear Carry to attend to him. The birth of this dear infant awoke up all the old memories of the time when my own precious William Fulke saw the light, and I became a mother. I could hardly realise that 36 years had passed away, and that I was now a grandmother.

Dearest Carry's recovery was most rapid. She was able to nurse her child and had not a single drawback. On the fifth day, feeling so well, she was allowed to get on the sofa and insisted on her husband's driving me in his phaeton to see Canterbury cathedral and Battle Abbey. It was a lovely morning, and she was wheeled to the window to see us start. Johnny

Lane, Pawlett's young brother, was at Tongswood and sat behind with the groom, I sitting with Pawlett.

A few miles from Canterbury we had to cross a railway, and just as we got on it one of the horses was frightened and began to kick. Pawlett bid the groom get down and go to his head, when the gate keeper cried out, 'Don't stop, the Express is coming!' so Pawlett whipped the horses and they started off, in fact bolted, and Pawlett lost all control over them and over *himself*, for he threw down the reins and jumped out, as did his brother Johnny, and let me alone to my fate (for the groom had not caught up with us). I seized the reins hoping to guide them straight along the road till they were tired and might stop of their own accord, as I knew it would be madness in me to attempt to jump out as it was a very high phaeton. However, in spite of all my efforts they rushed up a steep bank, the near horse fell down, struggling in vain to rise, and the other began kicking violently. Most wonderful to say the carriage was not upset.

I sat still till Pawlett and the groom and Johnny came, and then I did cry, 'Oh! One of you help me to get out,' and I was indeed thankful to find myself safe on my legs. Pawlett was in a dreadful way when he found the pole broke and the front of his phaeton kicked to pieces, and his best horse with both knees badly broken, and otherwise injured.

Johnny ran back to the gate keeper for help but the good-for-nothing man refused all aid, and had actually told a falsehood in saying 'the Express is coming' for it was not even due. We had to wait till some men fortunately were coming on the road and adjusted us, and to make a long story short the pole was tied together and, with one horse, and leading the lamed animal, we had to go at foot's pace to Canterbury, and then the carriage went to the coach makers and the horses went back to Tongswood. I gave a particular charge to the groom not to say a word about the accident lest dear Carry should hear of it.

On the 18th I left Tongswood, slept in London and got to

dear old Charlecote the next day. Mr Thomas came to us and to our astonishment, and I may add sorrow, told us he was engaged to Miss Desirée Urtot, a Belgian prima donna. We had seen and heard her at the opera when we were in London, she had a magnificent voice and a very commanding figure, but was exceedingly plain. In fact I had told Mr Thomas one day when he was giving me a harp lesson that she had the face of a lion. He laughed and said, 'She is certainly not handsome, but what a voice.'

Spencer, who was in the room, said, 'I suppose she makes lots of money, I advise you to make up to her. Ah! I see a rose bud in your coat! Did she give it to you?'

'Yes,' he replied, 'and I think she likes me, and her uncle, a portrait painter with whom she is staying, hinted as much to me; but a prima donna would never do for my wife.'

This conversation had only taken place two months ago, so we were surprised at the result. He told me how it had come to pass. The uncle had been constantly inviting him to meet her and he certainly thought her, independent of her musical talents, a very superior person in her conversation etc., and one morning when he called, the uncle showed him a charming picture he had just finished of her and said to him, 'Now Thomas, you must sit to me for your portrait was a pendant to it, for I must tell you my niece has fallen so desperately in love with you that her whole happiness depends on you', and he left him alone, and Desirée came into the room and, shortly after—he hardly knew how—they were betrothed.

After he left I often heard from him and he mentioned Desirée with the greatest affection but did not at all approve her surroundings and saw many things in a stage life to shock his sensitive feelings. He determined that she should give it all up when she became his wife.

In September we went to Plasgwyn to visit my youngest brother, dear Willy, who was married and rented the place from Lord Vivian. We met there Mr and Mrs Weldon who had not long been married and were the most loving couple. I did not care for him but was charmed with her, she was so clever, so fascinating, so pretty, such eyes—so full and bright—and had such a lovely voice and carried you away with whatever she sang as you heard every word. I can never forget 'The Miller's Daughter'; so graphic, I saw it all as well as heard it.

One morning she did not come down, he said she was not quite well so he would take her up some breakfast, and when the gentlemen went out shooting he declined going as he could not leave her. After luncheon we ladies went out walking and she went with us, so did he. When we came in I was so amused for she told him to take off her dirty boots and fetch her slippers, and he did as she bid him. Afterward I happened to be in the room alone with him, and laughed and said 'What a pattern husband you are!' When he replied, 'Oh! I can never be good enough to her for you must know she ran off with me and left all her comforts for me, for I am a poor man, now, at least, though I hope by and by to be well off.' He could not let her out of his sight, yet now they hate one another, are separated, and he has tried to put her in a lunatic asylum.

After the Weldons went, my sister-in-law Arabella Williams took me one afternoon—though it was very stormy and cold—in her little pony carriage (accompanied by her little dog that always followed her everywhere) for a drive along the sea shore. As the tide was out, we went on the sands very far till we came to a broad sort of channel. I said to Arabella, 'You will not attempt to go through that water?'

'Ah yes, why not?' and she whipped the pony and made him step in, which he did not like at all.

After we had gone some way, I said to the coachman who was sitting behind, 'Is it safe, for I am quite giddy?'

'Well indeed,' he replied, 'I feel like a swim but I think the missus had best go back.' Now he was Welsh and could not speak much English. The water was already up to the pony carriage wheels and just coming in to wet our feet; but it was too late, for I had no sooner spoken than the pony sunk and it almost disappeared. The coachman cried, 'Oh! Dear, dear what shall become of us! We have got into the quicksilver' (he meant quicksands). He got out and undid the traces, when the pony struggled and gave a violent plunge and freed himself, and trotted off towards the shore. The pony carriage was sinking deeper and the coachman said to me, 'Get on my back, and let me save you.'

I said, 'Save your mistress first.' However Arabella insisted that I should be first and he would return for her, and as there was no time to be lost, I jumped out of the carriage on to his back. I could not help screaming with laughter, for the man was very short, the wind was blowing a perfect hurricane and my red cloak was flapping about like a great sail, and then over my head preventing me from seeing where he was taking me. And he, so stupid, instead of making for the shore like the pony, was going towards the sea. I found my legs go plump into the water, and indeed far above my knees, and the little coachman cried out, 'Oh! Mrs Lucy, we are got fast in the quicksilver again,' and he sunk up to his chin; at which I let go my hands, which were around his neck, and dropped like an enormous bird on the water. I said, 'Quick, swim and save yourself,' which he quickly did, crying out 'The Lord have mercy! We are drowning! Oh! Mrs Lucy!'

I expected every moment I should indeed be drowned, but my crinoline held me up from sinking overhead. I tried my best to follow the coachman to the pony carriage but the more I struggled to get along, the more difficult I found it. It seemed as if my legs were in a *pease pudding*, and there I must stick.

I saw the man take Arabella out of the pony carriage and carry her to the shore. He then returned for me, and with tremendous struggling I got to the pony carriage, but was so exhausted I could get no further. So the good little man a second time took me on his back, and this time carried me safe on shore. Some men on one of the hills saw us and came to help us in our distress; after much pulling with their united strength they got the little carriage out of the quicksands, caught the pony and we drove back to Plasgwyn.

When we got home poor Arabella was quite ill from the fright and went into hysterics. I was so thoroughly wet that neither my boots nor stockings would come off. Young (my maid) pulled and pulled till I declared she would drag my legs off; and she laughed, and I laughed so, that Arabella's maid came to enquire if I was in hysterics and could she bring me sal volatile, or do anything for me? I said, 'Oh, no thank you. I am only laughing, because I expect my boots will never part from my stockings or my stockings from my legs.' At last Young got one boot off, and after resting awhile, for she was so tired (it was such hard work, for the sea water seemed to have glued all three together), she pulled the other off. They were new boots which I had worn for the first time and they were entirely spoiled, so shrivelled up that no foot could get into them again as I was obliged to roast my legs to dry my stockings before they would come off.

There was a dinner party that evening, and my friend the little coachman waited at table and when I looked at him I could hardly believe that I had been on his *back*, and when I told Spencer he roared with laughter, and said, 'Impossible! He could never have carried you!'

On the 18th the dear Pawlett Lanes took leave of us all and were to start for India on the 22nd: he was ordered out to join his regiment and my most dearly loved Carry would accompany him. The precious infant Aymer came to Charlecote with his nurse, Hunt, as his dear parents had the good sense and self-denial to leave him in the care of the Fitzhughs.

About this time Mr Thomas came also to Charlecote, having left Desirée at Dresden. She wished him to take a house in London ready for their marriage. He seemed sadly out of spirits and confided to me that he was not happy, that he had seen many things in an operatic life to shock his sensitive feelings and he also felt that his own brilliant career as a harpist would be lost in hers. He had quite made up his mind therefore that when she was his wife she must give up the stage, and had told her so, but she signified as much that she could not.

He had a long talk with Spencer about his future prospects, and Spencer, as well as myself, advised him to write and get a positive answer from her whether she could, or whether she would, comply with his wish and abandon the stage before he troubled to seek for a house. He did write but she put off from time to time making up her mind. She had a hard struggle between her great love for him and her devotion to her art, but the latter prevailed and the match was broken off in the month of June.

Meanwhile in India, dear Carry had several frightful illnesses and we were terribly alarmed and feared for her survival. In the spring of 1861 she had tetanus, a fearful spasmodic disease peculiar to India. She lay at the point of death for weeks. When she was able to hold a pen, she wrote,

'My dear, dear Mamma, you will be comforted to hear I am gaining strength, though not flesh. Poor dearest Pawlett has been almost beside himself with grief thinking he might lose me at any minute, his kindness and devotion to me is quite indescribable.'

Then in July 1862 she had a terrible premature confinement of a son still-born. When she was sufficiently recovered, Pawlett got leave to move from Peshawar to Murree, a hill station, and from there I received a letter from her, dated Murree, August 24th 1861:

'My own darling Mamma, your most dear letter by the last mail gave us the greatest joy. Thank you my dearest Mamma for being so good and kind, writing so often. Since I have been here I have been almost helpless from weakness. You know, dearest Mamma, in general I do not want much waiting upon, but I am glad to say I have an Ayah who is always at my "beck and call" and never keeps me waiting a moment. Dear Pawlett never leaves me excepting to attend his duties at the barracks and dine at Government House, as he is in duty bound. I am so truly thankful to think he finds his home such a happy one that he never cares to leave his little wife for other society.

I am obliged to be very strict with all our Indian servants, they require so much looking after or one's household would never be kept in nice order. Pawlett gives me great credit for my management. I keep the accounts, pay the servants' wages, and he manages the stable department. We have a very good cook and we have two cows and I see to the milking and churn the butter in bottles. I attend to my garden and poultry and we are going some day to have a green goose when we get our apples from Cashmere. They call this the land of apricots.

In September she had another frightful attack of tetanus while at Murree. Happily her husband was with her. Three doctors attended her, her sufferings were almost beyond belief. They cut off all her beautiful hair, blistered her poor head and nearly her whole body, and applied such hot bottles to her feet and legs that they made them perfectly raw. For one whole day, the doctors, having given up all hope, thought she was dead. In short, her return to life was a miracle. It was now decided that when she was able to travel she must return to England. Then she wrote:

'I am very much delighted at the thoughts of seeing you all again my darling Mamma, and wild with joy when I think of holding my precious child in my arms after an absence of two years.'

On the 1st April 1863 I went to London by the early train, having received a letter from Pawlett saying he and his dear wife should be at Holloway's Hotel in Dover Street that morning. When I arrived I found they were not come so I stationed myself at the window to watch every vehicle as it drove to the door, but hour after hour passed and they did not arrive. At last I went to bed in the most restless state of misery, and was up with the lark next morning hoping for a telegram

or letter, but none came. Again I watched at the window. I
started at every sound, at every footfall. Oh, what a tantalising
place is an hotel in which you are waiting for some dear friend!
All the talk, noise and business going on and no one caring or
troubling themselves about you.

I left in despair by the latest train to return home, and as I got
out at Warwick the station master said, 'There is a telegram for
you.' It was from Pawlett saying, 'Pray, come back, we have
arrived.' I almost cried with vexation for there was no return
train so late. Next day being Good Friday, I waited till
Saturday, when Spencer went to London with me, and my
past anxious misery was forgotten in the joy of clasping my
beloved Carry once again to my heart. But I was shocked to
find her but the shadow of her former self. That same afternoon the darling came back with us to Charlecote. Pawlett left
us at Reading to go to his parents at Badgemoor.

On the 7th I took my dear Carry to Plas Power. The
meeting between the sisters and precious little Aymer was
most touching. He was in Emily's arms when she came into
the room, with his dear little face nestled close to hers. She
then said to him, 'Here is your very own Mamma, go and kiss
her!' He instantly ran to her, put his arms round her neck,
kissed and kissed her again and again, and said, 'Baby has two
Mammas now.'

Carry went to join her husband at Badgemoor soon after,
taking little Aymer with her, and I returned to dear Charlecote. On the 25th Lord Paget came to stay with us and to my
astonishment Lady Hartop with her girls appeared at luncheon. They had come all the way from Four Oaks. It was a
lovely day and I was so pleased to see them and so fortunate
that I happened to be at home. I was expecting Lady Warwick
and her children to tea and to spend the afternoon. (The dear
boys used to enjoy a row on the river and to have tea in my
little cottage.) When they arrived I went to meet them in the
hall, and seeing a fly in the court, I wondered who it could be.
Lady Warwick said it was her aunt, Lady Ruthven, and that I

would think it so strange, but the truth was that just as they were starting the old lady drove up in a Leamington fly to the castle and Lady Warwick told her she was so sorry she could not receive her then as she was going to Charlecote by appointment.

'Oh!' she exclaimed, 'the very place of all others I wish to see. I will follow you.'

'So, dear Mrs Lucy, what could I say, you must think it so odd. I must tell you she is peculiar, and don't be surprised should you hear her talking quite loud to herself.'

I rushed into the court and handed the old soul out of the fly and said I was delighted to make the acquaintance of any one belonging to my dear friend Lady Warwick. We had a very merry tea and the good old aunt seemed to enjoy herself. I took her to see the pictures in the drawing room and she admired them immensely, and regretted there was not half time to see all the beautiful things. Then all of a sudden she said to me, 'You are expecting the Leighs from Stoneleigh next week, are you not?'

I replied, 'Yes, on Tuesday.'

'Well then, I should like to come and meet them and see more of your beautiful things.'

I answered, 'I should be charmed but the house will be quite full as a number of young men are coming to us for a cricket match between Staffordshire and Charlecote to take place in our park.' But counting all the names I found the Ebony room in the north wing would be vacant, only I said I feared she would object to it as there would be no ladies on that side; it would be entirely occupied by gentlemen.

'Oh! I shall not mind them! Let me see it.' So I took her upstairs and when she saw it she cried out, 'Charming! Splendid! A bed room fit for a queen. I will come.' And accordingly she made her appearance on the Tuesday.

The next morning the weather was lovely and we ladies all went to look at the match being played, and Lady Ruthven seemed to enjoy it as much as the youngest of us. I do not remember the names of all the cricketers but I *do* remember that Charlecote beat Staffordshire. I was so amused that evening when about eleven o'clock we wished the gentlemen good night and Lady Leigh with her girls was gone to her room and I was going to take Lady Ruthven upstairs to hers, she said to me, 'Stop, I should like to go into the library and have another look at those young men, for I do not know when I have seen so many very good looking ones.' I said, 'Oh, no! It would never do, they would be so astonished,' but she would have her way and into the room we went.

Spencer started and said, 'Whatever brings you here, what do you want?'

I replied, 'Lady Ruthven wishes to have another look at you all as she declares she has never seen such a handsome set of young men before.' On which they burst out laughing and stood in a line drawn up before her. And then I got her away to bed.

She herself was the very plainest woman that could be seen. Her complexion was lead colour (from having taken zinc), eyes light and small, and her nose enormous and of a purple dye. She was very clever and drew beautifully. She was such an early riser, was up before any of us and was out of doors taking views of the place. She invited me to visit her in the autumn in Scotland which I did, making other delightful visits on the way, which I shall describe.

I started on the 14th of September with my maid Young and we got to Edinburgh that night and slept at Douglass' Hotel. The next day, after making some purchases in the town, I went in a fly (for which I paid 16s 6d) a distance of about 10 miles to Hopetoun where I spent ten most charming days. Hopetoun is a palace and the grounds and views are most extensive and beautiful, and the house itself is full of exquisite china and glorious pictures.

Amongst others staying there were Colonel and Lady Jane Dundas. The first day the Colonel took me in to dinner and the conversation happened to turn upon beauty and ugliness, and different people were mentioned as being ugly or handsome. Then I said the very plainest person I knew was Mr Nisbett Hamilton, he had the face of a bull dog, and turning to Colonel Dundas said, 'Do you know him?'

'Yes,' he replied, 'for he is my brother.' I was horrified but could not unsay what I had said, but looking the Colonel full in the face stammered out, 'How could I suppose that you, so unlike, could be related to him, so pray forgive me.' And he did forgive me and we became great friends.

One afternoon Ethel (Lady Hopetoun) drove me in her pony carriage with her beautiful pair of piebald ponies to Dalmeney Park a short distance from Hopetoun. The house is modern and I did not admire it. You pass the ruins of the old one which was situated close to the water's edge. I can just remember about the time I married that the Countess of Rosebery of that day had eloped with a baronet whose name I forget. He came in a boat and she got out of the window and ran off with him—her husband was distracted and caused the whole of the house to be pulled down excepting the wing in which was the window from which she made her escape, and it forms a very picturesque ruin, partially covered with ivy.

Lord Hopetoun, though very clever, was not at all a polite host. He never troubled to entertain his guests, but left them to themselves. He breakfasted early and lone and when we came down he was generally standing with his back before the fireplace and took no notice of anyone except myself with whom he shook hands and said 'good morning'. His wife too rarely made her appearance till breakfast was over. Indeed she often did not get up till twelve or one o'clock. She sang charmingly every evening, either by herself or duets with her pretty sister. He used to take a book and sit in a corner and read till he went off to bed.

From Hopetoun I went to visit the Hays at Duns Castle. Mrs Hay was the sweetest and kindest of women, but her husband was a very rough diamond. He took such a quantity of snuff that I am sure it dulled his intellect, and it was quite unpleasant to be his neighbour at dinner, which was usually my lot, for he kept his snuff box on the table, next to me, and often dropped some, after taking a pinch, on the cloth. So I told Mrs Hay and the girls that I would hide it some day during dinner. They all laughed and said, 'Impossible for his eye or his hand are always upon it.' There was a picture of his grand-mother over the mantelpiece and he was very fond of telling a long history of it. So one day at dinner when he had helped the soup and taken his usual pinch of snuff and laid the box down, I said, 'Oh, Mr Hay do tell Sigr Lorenzo that story about your beautiful grandmother.' So he turned to look at the picture and began its history and I whipped the snuff box into my pocket like an experienced pickpocket.

When the joint was put on the table he wanted again to feed his nose and, not finding his box, said, 'How is this, surely it was here a moment ago! Here, Thomas, look under the table, it must have dropped down.' So I had to stand up and the footman rummaged about, but of course in vain. He then sent another footman to search in his dressing room, and when the man came back without finding it, he worked himself up into a rage and I won't here repeat the language he used. I told him he was much better without his horrid snuff, which made him more angry still. Dear Mrs Hay begged of me to give him his box before bed time or she should have no peace, so I did, and feared he would have been furious with me. But no, when I told him how I had taken it, he could not help laughing.

On the 24th I went to Winton Castle, Lady Ruthven's, and there met Mr Thomas. The old lady was all kindness and made herself most agreeable. She had a Greek butler—Angelo by name, who had lived for many years as cook during Lord Ruthven's life, and she had a great regard for him as her husband had been very partial to him, but I was amazed at his insolent behaviour to her. He would come into the room if he wanted 'The Times', and take it from her if she was reading it. One day she ordered her barouche at half past two o'clock to drive Mr Thomas and me to make some calls, and when the carriage came round Mr Thomas and I were ready but Lady Ruthven was not down. Angelo said in his broken English to me, 'You get in. What shame my Lady keep you waiting. I soon fetch her down, she never ready.' And up stairs he went, and presently brought her, pushing her along, and, taking her by the shoulders, positively shoved her into the carriage. She did not speak but looked daggers at him and her nose became a deeper purple. I was quite shocked. After we had gone about a mile and Mr Thomas was telling her some story about Russia she suddenly shouted, 'Beast, beast!' Mr Thomas looked at me and was silent, wondering what he had said to displease her so. I too was startled and could not think what had occurred to so excite her, but the mystery was soon solved when she muttered again, 'Beast, that beast Angelo—to push me into the carriage!'

The next morning's post brought me a letter from Pawlett Lane telling me that my dear Carry had had a narrow escape of being burnt to death. Just before undressing to go to bed she caught her lace sleeve in the candle and in a moment was all in a blaze. She rang the bell and Hunt her maid soon came and, taking a blanket off the bed, wrapped it round her, and so extinguished the flames. But her arm was dreadfully burnt. This put me into a terrible state of anxiety and I left Gosford and all my hospitable Scotch friends and got home on the 2nd October.

It made my heart ache to see how much my dear Carry was suffering from the terrible burns on her arm, but she was so patient, she never complained. At the end of the month, Pawlett returned to India to join his regiment and it was a sad and last parting for they never saw each other again. Four months after that his gentle, loving, faithful wife was taken from an earthly to a heavenly home.

Two weeks after Pawlett's departure, Spencer gave a ball so that dear Carry might see her old friends of other days, and she thoroughly enjoyed it. I never saw her look more charming. She was so beautifully dressed, she wore the exquisite beetle's wing dress which Pawlett gave her in India.

On the 17th of November she went with little Aymer to stay with the Stuart Lanes in London where she consulted Dr Tyler Smith and engaged him to attend her in her confinement which she expected in April. She was wonderfully well and strong, considering her situation, but had suffered from head aches ever since her illness in India. In February she left London and went with Baby to the Fitzhughs at Plas Power. She wrote me a long letter the next day in which she said, 'I slept well after the journey last night, and have been sitting in the library all day, for there is a heavy fall of snow. I had such a splitting head ache when I last wrote to you from the Stuart Lanes that I nearly fainted away over my letter and cannot remember what I said to you. God bless you my darling Mamma, no end of love to you all, your most loving Carry.'

On Monday 29th February my loving Carry, with little Aymer, went to Boddlewyddan with the intention of staying about ten days and then I was to have taken her to London for her confinement. But oh! How little do we know what a day will bring forth and how in the midst of life we are in death!

There was a large party staying at her Uncle Hugh's* on Friday the 4th March. She went out for a drive in the open carriage with Lady Williams, played on the piano that evening and delighted everyone, appearing as well as usual and went up stairs about half past ten o'clock. Before she went to bed she began to write a letter to me (found in her blotting book unfinished, and which I received when the dear hand that penned it was cold in death). It ran thus:

'My darling Mamma. I was so pleased to get your dear letter this morning. My head has ached almost incessantly lately so I do not think Dr Tyler Smith's medicine is agreeing with me. I have just written to him to tell him so and hope he may think of something to relieve me. The swelling of all my limbs and even my face is very painful, however I must bear

*By this time Brother had died and been succeeded by Hugh, now Sir Hugh Williams.

it patiently a little time longer. Aunt Williams has comforted me greatly and thinks it nonsense to go to London too soon, so I am sure if we go the beginning of April it will do perfectly.'

The next morning, about nine o'clock, Hunt took Aymer to say his prayers and she heard him for the last time say, 'God bless dear Papa and Mamma!' She told Hunt she had had a very restless night but she was quite cheerful, had her breakfast in bed and told Hunt to take her dear child down stairs as she felt rather sick so would rest for an hour or so, then go out for a walk and, afterwards, would finish her letter.

Hunt had not left the room more than ten minutes when the housemaid called her back saying Mrs Lane was very sick. She brought up a quantity of bile and complained of great pain in her head. Hunt went for Lady Williams who came immediately and said, 'Dear Carry, shall I send for the Doctor?'

'Oh no!' she replied, 'I shall be well presently.'

However, her aunt sent off to Denbigh for Dr Turnour, but before he arrived she had five convulsion fits, blood had flown from her nose, mouth and ears, and she was insensible.

Dr Turnour applied mustard plasters to her neck which roused her in a slight degree. She turned herself a little and muttered, 'Lord have mercy upon me! Have mercy upon me,' and never spoke again. In about half an hour after, she had a violent convulsion, frightful to witness, and she died at seven o'clock.

On Sunday morning about six o'clock I heard my door open and Young (my maid), coming hastily to my bedside, crying, said, 'Oh! My dear mistress, prepare yourself for dreadful news! Sir Hugh Williams' footman is just arrived from Boddlewyddan to say Mrs Pawlett Lane is dead.'

'Dead,' I cried. 'How! When? No, it cannot be!' My heart felt bursting with agony and terror. I fell back on my pillow and, weeping bitterly, prayed to God to support me under his awful and grievous burthen of misery.

Carry

Spencer and Tina shortly after their marriage in 1865

*Above: Tina wearing the dress in which she was presented at Court
Opposite: Spencer in middle age*

Mary Elizabeth at the age of sixty-three

Mary Elizabeth's grandchildren, Ada and Linda Lucy

Ada and Linda; 'their lives passed from childhood to adolescence without a ripple.'

Mary Elizabeth, aged 80, in her boudoir, with her harp

MEL's boudoir remains unchanged today

*Ada **Fairfax-Lucy** and four of her six children. Brian (left) was to marry Alice, daughter of John Buchan (Lord Tweedsmuir), who introduces these memoirs.*

Tom and Emily came to mingle their tears with ours and Hunt brought poor little Aymer from Boddlewyddan. On the 11th, my brother Hugh, Mr Lane and his sons came to attend the darling's funeral which was to take place the next day, for at my request she was to be laid beside her own dear father and brothers in Charlecote church.

The preceding night was to me terrible, and I can never forget it. I knew the hearse with her remains would arrive in the very early morning and the anguish in my heart kept me all night with unclosed eyes, as it were, in the 'valley and shadow of death'. At length I heard a heavy rumbling sound under my window, whilst a thrush was warbling his sweetest note on one of the cedars on the green and the gateway clock chiming an hour which, for very faintness, I could not count. Daylight was just breaking. Oh gracious God! How I longed to rush out of bed and open the window and see the coffin containing my darling Carry being carried into the house. But I felt I could not move, a sharp pain ran through my whole frame. I could not stir, I could not cry, and for a time life seemed to have gone from me.

On the very day she was buried a letter arrived from Pawlett. It was dated February 7th. (He generally wrote six or seven pages by every mail as she did to him.)

'My own Darling Wife. Last night brought letters from you for which I must truly thank you. What a joy it is to receive letters from you. I do feel very unmannish when I get yours. I always sit very still for a minute holding them tight in my hand before I open them. There is such an intense delight in knowing that you hold safe in your hand what you have been looking forward to for so many days. I have read your dear letters over twice already, and I do bless God for having given me such a loving wife, and my daily fervent prayers are that in due time you may be restored to me again. There is nothing on earth I would take in exchange for you. What would our little boy be without you?

My mother writes to tell me that she has never seen you looking better, and such a blessing that you are able to take such long walks.

I am now fancying you walking along the beach, with Amy holding your hand and Hunt carrying the new Baby in its long white robes after you. You are my life. God bless and preserve you, my darling wife, through all your troubles and make you the happy mother of another child.'

Another letter, March 24th, from Umballa.

'My own Darling dear wife. I am expecting every day, my comfort, a letter from you. You are my bright spot. To you I look for comfort and happiness and when your letters tell me you know and feel this, that my happiness comes from you, I get cheered up. You are the little being whose approval and love I covet.'

The opening and reading these loving letters from poor Pawlett to his dear wife, thinking her to be alive when she was gone, was to me heart-rending. Finally, on the 23rd May I received a letter from him, part of which I here copy.

Umballa, Punjab, April 19th. 'Dearest Mam. On the 14th I learnt by telegraph of that loss which for the rest of my life I can never cease to feel. Oh, dearest Mam, if I could but tell you the void it has made in my life! I never did anything or thought or planned anything but always said to myself, "What will my Darling think of it?" And now to know that all this is gone, that I can never write to her, never hear from her, never see her. Oh God, it is very dreadful! She was my comfort: whenever I was unhappy her little hand would steal into mine, and her dear face tell me how she shared my grief, and I am never to have this again, and the rest of my life is to be alone.'

126

1865–1870

The Old Order Changes

Henry Spencer was a kindly man who liked sharing the good things that came his way. He acted out the principle of limiting his desires according to his ability and opportunity to fulfil them. His desires were not, for his time, excessive: hunting (he became Master of the Warwickshire Hunt), shooting (he was the best shot in three counties), good dinners, good wine (his Château Margaux was famous) and agreeable company. His inherited Tory-ism was that of all decent-thinking country landlords of his class and standing in the County, who desired only to go on leading the life and holding the opinions to which they had been born. He might have claimed for himself that he would be perfectly satisfied to occupy his grandfather's worn armchair after a day out with hounds, to sit at the head of a table that accommodated his friends and watch them enjoying his wine, to walk with a gun across his own land at dusk when the duck were flighting, to visit his horses in the warm breath of the Charlecote stables, to entertain his tenants with Charlecote venison eaten off china bearing the family crest. Had he given the matter any thought he might have added that the young wife he meant to have must be a 'stunner' and also have the good sense not to cross his obsessively loving and dominating mother, or his peace would be in ruins.

On February 18th, 1865, Mr, Mrs and Miss Campbell of Monzie in Perthshire dined at Charlecote. It was the first time I had seen Mrs Campbell or her daughter. Mr Campbell I knew

127

slightly as he had once dined and slept here when we happened to have a tenants' ball, which he seemed to enjoy as much as the farmers, and danced away with all the prettiest girls till morning. Little did I think that his daughter would be the future mistress of dear old Charlecote! At the ball he asked Spencer if he would get me to call on his wife in Leamington, which I did, and then asked them to dinner.

It was Tina's first dinner party and she was not at all shy and was perfectly self-possessed, whilst her mother was quite the contrary. Lord Conyers, as he was taking me in to dinner, said, 'Who is that stunner of a girl?'

'Miss Campbell,' I replied. She was dressed in white muslin with a scarlet sash and wore a gold chain with a diamond cross on her neck. I thought she was a very fine girl, with a lovely complexion, good eyes and rich brown hair. We had a great deal of music in the evening as Mr Thomas was with us, and he and I played harp duets etc. I asked Tina to play, but she said she could not. I saw at once that she did not care much for music.

After that evening Spencer often talked of her, and they met occasionally at the meets when she rode with her father, but she did not hunt. About the middle of May we took a house in London, 57 Grosvenor Street, for the Season and Spencer said, 'We must take up the plate and give dinners, and you must assemble all the nicest girls, for me to find a wife, as you are always telling me it is time I should get married.' So on the 16th, Parsons, Horton and other servants, with the service of plate, went to 57 Grosvenor Street and we were to follow on the 19th. That same afternoon (the 16th) Spencer drove to Leamington to call on Mr Campbell and see him on some subject connected with sport. He did not come back to dinner, and the next morning when I went into his room, with the intention of joking him about Miss Campbell, I found his bed had not been slept in. Tina's image like a flash of lightning rose before me, and I quitted the room, feeling that Charlecote, dear Charlecote, would not long be what it was, nor what it had been—my home, the home which for so many long years had held my heart and soul.

It was a lovely morning and after breakfast I went out to busy myself in the garden. About five o'clock in the afternoon I was seated on a stool directing Peyton (the gardener) how the flowers should be arranged in the different beds in the court, thinking to myself, well, it is perhaps for the last time, when I heard the sound of a carriage and saw it was Spencer's dog cart. I flew to him and at once saw by the joyous smile on his countenance what had happened. We neither of us spoke till we got into the house, then he clasped me in his arms and said, 'Tina is mine.'

'God bless your choice,' I cried, then we kissed and kissed each other again and again, exchanged many true words of love and affection, and a few tears mingled joy and sorrow. 'Tell me then,' I said, 'how you came to propose so suddenly?'

'Well, Campbell pressed me to remain to dine and sleep, and at dinner time Tina, who sat next to me, looked so charming, and after she and her mother had left the room her father began to talk about her and say that she had many admirers etc. but none that he approved, and then said a good deal more which excited me as I had had several glasses of champagne, so then I said, "Perhaps I should have no chance," on which he seized my hand, said, "Are you serious?" "Yes." "Then my boy you have my full consent, go and ask her." By this time it was too late, the ladies had retired to rest.

'Next morning I went into the drawing room and found Tina alone, seated at the piano. I asked her what she was playing. She said, "Le Chemin de Paradis." (She was indeed on the road to an earthly paradise.) "Well, stop for a moment, I have something to say to you. Do you think we should suit each other? In short, will you be my wife?" She blushed and said, "Yes." Now dearest Mamma, fly, be quick, change that old garden dress, make yourself nice for Mr and Mrs Campbell and their two daughters Tina and Lucy will be here at six o'clock, and you must get up a good dinner for them.'

'Well,' I exclaimed, 'You have often told me to do impossible things in a minute, but this beats them all! You forget that Horton, her two kitchen maids etc., and Parsons and all the plate, are gone to London, and that there are only a few silver spoons and forks left out for us.'

'Never mind, never mind, you dear Mam, you must manage all that, but make haste, they will be here directly.'

So away I went to enquire what was in the larder and who could prepare the feast for the bride elect, then I flew upstairs to ring for Gates. No sooner was I dressed and made nice, and back in the court, than the iron gates were opened, and Mr Campbell in a light American carriage with a very handsome horse drove up to the front door with his wife and daughters.

'An undefined and sudden thrill which makes the heart a moment still' came over me as I hurried to receive them. We then went into the house and, soon after, dinner was ready. That most memorable dinner, never to be forgotten! The old proverb says 'Too many cooks spoil the broth', but here there was not one cook but too many maidens (the laundry maid, the dairy maid and two housemaids) who spoilt the broth. However, we were all too full of each other to care for the viands on the table and the champagne, 'that spring dew of the spirit', made us very happy. Mr Campbell got so excited that his tongue became smoother than oil in praise of his eldest daughter. Like Prospero he was ready to say to Spencer, 'Then here is my gift, and thine own acquisition; take my daughter. Do not smile at me that I boast her off. For thou shalt find she will outstrip all praise, and make it halt behind her.'

A few days later, on May 19th, we came to 57 Grosvenor Street as planned, and Mr and Mrs Campbell and their daughters came to London and established themselves at Fenton's Hotel in St James's Street. On Monday 23rd we dined with them. Next day too we dined at Fenton's Hotel and went to the play together. Soon I became almost worn out with driving backwards and forwards to St James's Street and Grosvenor Street. I really had not a moment I could call my own, and then all the love making—so pleasant to the lovers, but so stupid and wearisome to the lookers on! To select the trousseau was no trifle! Mrs Campbell, not knowing London, begged of me to get whatever was the right thing for her daughter. Mrs James of Hanover Square was my dressmaker and a very good one, so I took Tina, accompanied by Spencer, for the wedding dress, and others, to her. She was the type of milliner, so bland, so persuasive, to whom it was difficult to say no to anything she recommended.

'Oh! Miss Campbell will look so charming in this dove coloured silk, to travel in, you know; then here is a lovely blue silk which would so become her, then this pink is so exquisite it would so suit her fine complexion, and then oh! Miss Campbell must have this buff creation. I have just made a dress of the same for the Princess Mary of Cambridge. I make all her things, she is such a darling, only she is too large.' And so her tongue ran on till she would run you up such a bill that would make you cry out, as the Princess of Wales is reported to have done when she saw her first milliner's bill. 'Oh, Heaven forgive me for such extravagance!'

Then came the settlements; the lawyers were more difficult to manage than Mrs James. Mr Beith, the Scotch man, looked like a bird of prey and Mr Martin, the Englishman, a piece of old dried parchment (as if he had been nourished on old deeds instead of the milk of human kindness). The many questions they asked—and required to be answered; it was enough to puzzle Solomon himself and weary out the patience of Job.

On the 17th of June we all dined with Margaret Willoughby de Broke, and Tina was introduced to the relations. Spencer, who was anxious she should look her best, asked me to let Gates go to Fenton's Hotel and do her hair (as Gates was a perfect hair dresser). So of course I said, 'With pleasure', and Spencer was so charmed with the result—and we all thought it was so becomingly and beautifully done—that the next day he said to me, 'Do give up Gates to Tina, for you know she has not found a maid yet.'

'That is very hard on me for she suits me so well, and I hate changing. And how do you know, perhaps she will not wish the change either.'

He laughed and said, 'You will see, she will jump at it, for remember she came to you when you were mistress of Charlecote and she the great lady in the housekeeper's room.'

'Well,' I said, 'as you so much wish it, I will offer her Tina's place,' and I went up stairs and rang the bell; I confess with a heavy heart. Gates soon appeared and I said, 'Mr Lucy was so pleased with the way you dressed Miss Campbell's hair last evening that he wishes me to offer you her place as lady's maid. Mind, I have no wish to part with you, and shall be very sorry to lose you, but at the same time I think it right to tell you that I shall probably now have to take a small place, and very different from Charlecote, though I hope to make my servants happy and comfortable.'

She, without a moment's reflection, answered me thus: 'Surely what is good enough for you ought to be good enough for me, and I have no wish to leave you for any other mistress. But please thank Mr Lucy for his kind offer of the future Mrs Lucy's place.'

I was so touched that a tear trembled in my eye, and as I took her hand and pressed it, the tear fell upon it, and I flew down stairs and cried out, 'Gates will not exchange the old mistress for the young one.'

'Is that really true?' said Spencer.

'Yes, quite true.' (She has been with me now nearly 20 years and I hope will live with me as long as I live. She is the best maid I have had and is invaluable to me in illness.)

The wedding day was fixed for the 5th July, and as it was absolutely necessary for me to get to Charlecote beforehand to arrange and settle everything for the reception of the bride and bridegroom, I went down on the 1st of July—unfortunately the only day I could be spared, but, happily, its peculiar sadness was unremembered by all save myself. Twenty years ago, on that day, 1845, I was made a widow; three years later on that same day, the 1st July 1848, I had mourned the loss of my dearly beloved first-born son.

I travelled by rail in a carriage all alone and the many thoughts that crowded into my mind of the past, present and future so absorbed me that when I got to dear old Charlecote I almost forgot what I had come there for, nor did I realise my position till I went up stairs to take off my things and found my bed room was prepared for the future Mrs Lucy—the well remembered and well-worn furniture gone and replaced by new and all that was beautiful. So now, on 1st July 1865, I was called upon to give up forever the bedroom I had occupied as wife and widow 41 years, the bedroom in which three of my sons had been born—the never forgotten ones, to whom my heart cleaved. In that very room, when Spencer was 15 years old, his father had blessed him before he died. He laid his hand on his head and said, 'May God bless you! Yes and ever bless you! My dearest boy!' And indeed he had been blessed and may God still bless him and his young wife, I thought. He has been a good son to me, though the old saying is, 'My son is my son till he gets him a wife, my daughter is my daughter all the days of her life.'

The two days passed at dear Charlecote in preparing for my successor were certainly a trial, and nature would have her struggles, but still I rejoiced that Spencer's marriage was so near at hand, and the bright hope of his future happiness dispelled the clouds of my own gloomy thoughts and made me forget 'self' and how changed was my lot which had been cast on so fair a ground for so many years.

The 5th July (a Wednesday) was a morning without a cloud; the heat intense and the fuss and excitement at 57 Grosvenor Street, killing. At 12.30 the wedding party assembled in St George's Church, Hanover Square. The church was crowded. The bride, blooming with youth, modesty and grace, walked up the aisle on her father's arm, the cynosure of all eyes in the church. Her dress was beautiful, and Mrs James herself acted lady's maid on the occasion; so every fold sat in its right place.

It was of the richest white silk, covered with the most exquisite tunic of Brussels lace looped up the front with large bunches of orange flowers and true-lovers' knots of white satin. Her wreath of orange blossoms circled round her wavy hair and over all the finest Brussels lace veil which ere set off a marriage morning face.

The bridal party adjourned to the Clarendon Hotel where Mr Campbell gave a sumptuous wedding breakfast. Lord Charles Percy proposed the bride's health in a most eloquent and touching speech. The bridegroom returned thanks in a short but very good speech which came from his heart. Then followed many toasts, and the feast was ended and the guests dispersed. The bride changed her 'glorious apparel' for the dove coloured silk and the happy pair drove to Paddington Station, where I followed them in my barouche to see them off by the 3.40 train.

When they arrived at Warwick the enthusiasm was immense. Mr Chiltern, the station master, told me he never witnessed anything like it! They might have been the Prince and Princess of Wales. He had the greatest difficulty in keeping a clear road for Mr and Mrs Lucy to step into the Charlecote coach and four which was waiting for them. People lined the road all the way from Warwick to Charlecote, from the village to the entrance gates. Hundreds were assembled to hurrah with all their might, and many carriages full of neighbours and strangers were drawn along the side of the road to add to the welcome. A magnificent arch had been erected over the park gate, decorated with evergreens, roses and white lilies. It was just half past seven o'clock when a band of music struck up the air, 'The Campbells are Coming', and, amidst the most hearty cheers, the coach proceeded slowly down the avenue. All the tenantry, their wives, sons and daughters lined the road to the old Gateway, where on the roof streamed flags and banners with the arms of Lucy and Campbell. On their arrival at the Hall door they were received warmly by the Rev Hibbert who read an address from the tenantry. Spencer vainly endeavoured to reply: the court was filled with well wishers, and the hurrahs and cheers were so deafening, so hearty and so long, that the sound of his voice could not be heard.

The bride won the golden opinions of all the tenants' wives and daughters by untying her bonnet strings as soon as she alighted from the carriage that they might see the beautiful diamond and emerald locket—the prized wedding gift of the tenantry—put on that morning. And here I must say a word touching that locket. Spencer's tenants, having subscribed £124, requested me to select some piece of jewellery as a present from them to Spencer's bride, as a token of their regard for himself. I selected the locket at Hunt & Roskel's in Bond Street but, looking at the price marked £150, put it back expressing my regret that its value exceeded my commission by £26. Mr Hunt, after a short consultation with his other partner, said to me, 'We respectfully beg on this occasion to be considered as one of Mr Lucy's tenants and that you will take it for the £124.'

A booth 120 feet long was erected in the park at Charlecote, where dinner was laid for all the tenants who assembled at two o'clock to eat, drink and be merry. All the poor on the estate were feasted with as much as they could eat and drink. 600lb weight of meat was consumed, 200cwt of plum pudding, and upwards of 400 gallons of old ale, brewed at Charlecote, was drunk. There was a large tent for the wives and daughters of the tenants who met together to have tea and cake, and wine etc. All the women and village children had tea and plum cake, of which they cut 200lbs weight. Then followed all sorts of amusements and dancing till it grew dark when the revels were brought to a close by a grand display of fireworks. The weather was glorious and everything contributed to make this outdoor fête charming, and the wedding day of my dear son H. S. Lucy will not soon be forgotten. God bless him!

Nine months almost to a day my darling Ada was born. On Friday April 23rd Tina drove me in the phaeton to Warwick. The horses were very fresh, and pulled as they had not been out for a week (the weather having been so bad, with heavy snow for several days). It was a bitter cold afternoon, we went home round by Wellesbourne to leave a parcel, saw Colonel Campbell and had a few minutes' chat with him. As we turned the corner into Charlecote village, Tina said, 'Shall we call on Mr Pitt and tell him to be in the way if I should have to send for him?'

'What, do you feel ill?' I cried.

'Yes. I have had pains all the way but they are worse now.'

This put me in a proper fright, tho' I certainly did not think it possible that her hour of travail was so near. Mr Pitt's servant said he was out, and Tina would only allow a message to be left saying that if he was coming Charlecote way, in the evening, he might call. As we went under the gateway, the clock showed twelve minutes past five, and, at half past, the first Miss Lucy came into the world.

Immediately on our getting indoors I had sent off a note to Mr Pitt to come directly, but he did not get to us till ten minutes past six o'clock, when all was happily over. The young lady was so very fast that we could not get her Mamma's pretty red-striped stockings and dandy boots off and had barely time to lift her on to the bed before I had to act Dr Locock. [*The Queen's obstetrician. Mr Pitt was the local vet who also delivered babies.*] The baby was born with a caul which completely veiled her face and frightened me out of my wits, but I knew it must be removed immediately so I unveiled the little face, which was so deathlike I feared there was no life in the babe. I was in an agony for the arrival of Dr Pitt, whose astonishment was great to find that I had managed alone and had saved the life of the child.

Spencer and Tina were disappointed that they had not got a son, but I was so enchanted that a tiny girl was come all safe and right that I thought not of the greater joy. She surely must be something peculiarly good, clever, and charming to have come into the world on the same day of the month of April as the immortal Shakespeare.

Miss Ada Lucy was christened on the anniversary (the 5th July) of her parents' wedding day in Charlecote church by her great-uncle, John Lucy. The little darling was dressed in the same lace robe that her own Papa and all his brothers and sisters had worn when they were made Christians. She behaved charmingly.

I had now been living with my dear son and his wife for nearly twelve months in such perfect unity that they insisted on my making Charlecote my home, and I was only too too happy to continue at the dear dear old place, but I insisted that I must be allowed to build two rooms for myself so that I should never be in the way, and should feel thoroughly independent and 'commune with my own heart in my chamber and be still'.

A year later Tina gave birth to a second daughter (Constance Linda). Again I had to act doctor and nurse, and wash, dress, and feed this newborn babe, as I had done her little sister, now just eleven months old. Then on the 7th March 1870 about four o'clock p.m. on a Saturday, the third Miss Lucy, Sybil Mary, came into the world. This time the midwife was waiting to receive her. Tina sobbed bitterly and could not at all be reconciled to her disappointment that this new baby was not a boy. She kept crying and saying, 'Oh! What will Spencer say to me for having another girl?'

Spencer was out hunting and returned at six o'clock. Mary Elizabeth saw him first and told him he had a beautiful little daughter. He was vexed but was very considerate and did not express any regrets before his wife.

1871–1875

Here and There

Being a grandmother intensified Mary Elizabeth's already keen devotion to her family and was perhaps an even greater source of happiness than motherhood had been; not diluted by the need for discipline and correction that parents must exercise, with her grandchildren she could fully indulge her affectionate nature, and, like so many grandmothers before and since, she felt that hers were perfection. Her ambitions now were all for their future happiness, and she did not live to see it work out otherwise.

As the journals reach nearer the present, the entries increasingly take on the character of extracts from diaries—events occurring nearly a decade before seem to her to have happened yesterday. She continues to pay visits, describing with gusto all that she sees, but the visits nearly always centre round members of her own family. Like Queen Victoria, whom she so often brings to mind, Mary Elizabeth in old age remained, as in youth, steadfast in her attachment to those she loved and had loved, both living and dead; and her nature was shocked by less in others.

In July 1871 I was surprised to receive the following letter from Pawlett Lane to announce his intended second marriage. I had no idea he was thinking of any one; nor did it occur to me that the blank his dear wife and my darling Carry's death had left in his life, could ever be filled again.

Badgemoor. Dearest Mam, I must tell you of my engagement to Miss Bertha de Boulay of Dunhead Hall, Dorsetshire. They are a very good family and she has a fair fortune, but we shall not be very rich. Dearest Mam, I do hope this will not make you sorry, or hurt with me. You know that my love for darling Carry was deep and true.

I hope and believe Bertha will be a good and loving wife to me, and a loving mother to dear little Amie. She is naturally good and kind, it was quite a pleasing thing to see how beloved she is by all the poor people around. The neighbours too seem very sorry she is going away. My best love to you all, your very affectionate son Pawlett Lane. P.S. Lord and Lady Westminster, old friends of the de Boulays, are very warm in their good wishes.

In August, Spencer, Tina, Berkeley and his wife went to Courror, a grouse moor Spencer took annually in Scotland. The darling children went to Scotland on the same day with Hunt and Susan the nursery maid to their grand mamma Campbell in Inverness, and I was left all alone at old Charlecote; very lonely, but not dull, for I am always so full of occupation that time never hangs on my hands. But I did long, with an inexpressible longing, to hear again those dear children's voices echoing sweet and clear, and Ada, Ada, how I missed you! 'Nearer I seem to God when looking at thee.' This dear Ada, before she was two years old, could repeat the Lord's Prayer and that beautiful little hymn, 'Soft and quiet is the bed where I lay my infant head.'

Hunt wrote to me about the children from Scotland:

Inverawe. August 12th. The dear little Pets are so well and so happy. Miss Lucy said to Miss Linda, "This is a nice place, we will stay here for a long time. Poor Granny will be very lonely today but I do like this Scotland house so! And there are such dear little wild flowers." They are so enchanted with the heather and ferns and bring their baskets full of flowers every time they go out.

Miss Linda is so troubled when she sees the poor children going about without shoes or stockings, and says when she grows big, and has money, she will buy them some. The other day two little girls brought some bunches of heather to Miss Lucy and were going away when she called them back, and said, "Come here little girls, have you washed your hands? For they look so brown. Haven't you any soap?"

"No Mam, but indeed they are clean. We would not get flowers for you, little Mam, with dirty hands. It is the hot sun that makes them brown, and we have no nice gloves like you Mam."

On the 1st of September Pawlett was married to Bertha Dolbiac du Boulay. My dear Aymer went to the wedding and he told me that it was not such a grand one as his Uncle Spencer's and that the church was a disgrace and not fit to be called a church, so shabby and ready to tumble down. He thought he should like his new Mamma, but never love her as he had loved his own darling Mamma. And what's more, *I* never will, for I cannot see how she can be anything more than a connexion.

On the 18th September I went to Stoneleigh for a ball and Lord Leigh would insist on my opening it, dancing with him. I resisted all I could, reminding him that I was a grandmother, besides there were so many countesses and ladies of rank that he ought to open the ball with. But it was all in vain, so I had to do as he wished, and I danced down the middle and up again in the good old-fashioned Country Dance of about 20 couples or more and quite enjoyed it, but was not sorry to sit down.

On the 23rd I went with Emily to Mr Coffin, an American dentist, to have her tooth stopped. She insisted on his examining my teeth, so he put me in his horrid dentist chair and looked into my mouth and at first said all was right, but then began tapping like a woodpecker at every separate tooth, declared that he had found one double tooth that was going— or might go—and before I could get out of his clutches he gag'd me and set to work, positively cutting away half of it, and filling it up with gold which he knocked in with a small hammer till I thought he would hammer my brains out. He thumped and thumped for half an hour, when he was quite exhausted; and then his assistant hammered for another three quarters of an hour, and another young dentist came to look on, and exclaimed 'beautiful'! I was frantic, and when at last I did get out of the chair and looked in the glass and saw a nice white tooth (at least half of it) turned into gold, my rage knew no bounds. Yet I had to pay the wretch three guineas.

Mr Thomas came for Easter and I planted a cedar in front of the stables over poor Dandy, a favourite horse of Tina's, who was buried there. The Fitzhughs and Aymer came on the 12th and stayed till the 22nd. On Sunday 14th May 1872, on our return from church, we found a fourth Miss Lucy had been born, washed and dressed and was in Gates's lap. Ada, Linda and Sybil were enchanted with their new sister. Tina would be moved into Spencer's dressing room and had the window open and caught cold, and in a few days became dangerously ill, with congestion of the lungs, and violent sickness and fainting. Dr Carter from Leamington attended her and, thank God, she recovered rapidly.

On Sunday the 30th of July at half past two o'clock the little Joyce Alinore Lucy was christened in Charlecote church by the Reverend John Lucy who read the service beautifully for an old man of eighty years of age. She was dressed in the same lacy robe as her sisters, and behaved as well.

December 3rd [1872], Advent Sunday, will long be remembered as the day when a terrible fire partially destroyed Warwick Castle, wilfully set on fire by their own under butler. The noble Hall and private apartments were burnt to the ground. I drove over the following morning to see the sad spectacle and with my whole heart felt and sorrowed for the dear Warwicks. They were absent, having gone to London on the Saturday.

The grandchildren, little Eva and Sidney Greville, were there (at the Castle) and had a most narrow escape. The nurse was awoken by a cry of 'fire' at two o'clock in the morning, and had only time to snatch the two children out of their beds and rush through flames and dense smoke down the staircase. Five minutes afterwards the whole of the staircase fell in.

I went to the Warwick Arms where the dear little Eva and her brother had been taken in their night clothes. As soon as they saw me the darlings flew into my arms and told me how all their things were burnt. Happily most of the valuable treasures were saved, and the state apartments did not suffer. Lady Warwick told me that it was three weeks after the conflagration that they found it was their own servant who had done the deed. He had not long been in their service, and was a native of Birmingham. On the Saturday when they left the castle for London he asked the housekeeper's permission to have a friend of his to see the castle, and he came accordingly, and between them they stole every object of value in the private apartments, which the friend carried off. Then, to conceal the robbery, this under butler set fire to that side of the castle.

In February, for the Thanksgiving Day for the recovery of the Prince of Wales from a dangerous illness, typhoid fever, I went up to London, having received two cards to view the royal procession from a window in Oxford Street and never was more delighted in my life, for it was a glorious sight. The greatest marvel was the mighty mass of people who poured forth to fill streets, squares, windows, yes the very house tops. Oxford Street was enlivened from one end to the other with flags and banners of all colours and the ordinary lamps had been removed and replaced by coloured glass crowns and Prince of Wales' feathers. The mottoes were legion but the one which pleased me most was this, 'England today rejoices with the Queen. The Nation's and the Mother's heart are one.'

About three o'clock the shouts of welcome and waving of handkerchiefs indicated the approach of the Royal procession. The Lancers first came in view and detachments of the Guards and Hussars etc., then the Lord Mayor's State carriage and then nine of the Royal carriages. In the first seven were seated the different members of the Royal Household. In the eighth, the Master of the Horse the Marquis of Lorne, Prince George of Wales, Prince Leopold, Prince Arthur and the Duke of Edinburgh (these eight carriages were each drawn by four horses). In the ninth carriage, drawn by six horses in the most gorgeous harness glittering with gold, sat the Queen, Princess of Wales, the Prince of Wales, the little Prince Albert Victor of Wales, and Princess Beatrice. The Queen was dressed in black, the Princess of Wales in blue velvet, Princess Beatrice in mauve, the Prince in the uniform of a general with the orders of the Garter and the Bath. The mighty mass of people cheered with their whole heart not so much a queen and a prince as a mother and her son. The Prince appeared deeply moved by the enthusiasm of the crowd, and lifted his hat without cessation. I trembled lest he should take cold, for it was a bitter day with a north-east wind. As the royal carriage slowly wended its way past the window where I stood, my heart throb'd with emotion at the sight of the multitude paying their glad and heart felt message to their Queen and her son, on his recovery from a well-nigh mortal sickness.

In 1874 John Lucy died. He had entered his 85th year and he had a long illness to prepare him for his last journey. His narrow bed is alone by the side of a yew tree planted by himself in his own church yard at Hampton Lucy. My brother-in-law never was an active parish priest in the proper sense of the word; he belonged rather to a school of clergymen now rapidly passing away. He was much respected if not beloved by his parishioners as their rector for fifty years. He was bound to them and they to him by a link which length of time always rivets with a strength of which we are unaware till it is rent asunder.

All the household furniture, books, plate, china, etc., were to be sold by auction according to my old brother-in-law's will. The weather was most unfortunate, a severe frost and very deep snow preventing all our neighbours attending; so only brokers and Jews came, who would have got everything for little or nothing had not Spencer, Berkeley, the Fitzhughs and I, in spite of frost and snow, made a point of going each day, and not only bidding, but buying many an article we did not want simply to prevent it falling into the hands of these harpies for an old song. I never set out five days of such excitement, cold, and vexation of spirit; and I thought if the old Rector could have seen the dirty rabble in his once beautiful drawing room it would have driven him frantic—and more than all to have heard them bidding their shillings, yes! and *sixpennies*; and the auctioneer seated on one of John Lucy's nice tables, knocking down his choice and highly prized goods to people who he would not have deemed worthy to have looked at them. The total sold by auction realised £3,988.

Ever since Spencer's and Tina's marriage Mrs Campbell had entreated me with such kindness to visit her in Scotland, and so I determined to make the journey that August as my darling grandchildren, Joyce and Sybil, would be there too. (Spencer and Tina were also to be in Scotland at that time, but at Carour, shooting the grouse.)

So on the 18th August I started for Inverawe and went by the night rail train from Leamington. At Stirling I had to change for Tyndrum, where the journey by rail ended, and I had then to mount on the top of a Highland coach. Oh! such a vehicle! With four such miserable horses, and such tackle for harness; and such a coachman and guard, in scarlet coats stained black and blue by weather and dirt, very old worn drab breeches and marvellous boots. There were so many outside passengers that Gates and I had great difficulty in finding a seat. We fortunately had our waterproofs on for it was pouring with rain, but the inside of the coach looked so dirty that I preferred the chance of getting wet to sitting in it and being dry. There was only one occupant, a fat old Scotch minister.

We drove over such barren hills for miles and the ascent and descent were terrific, and most severe on the poor horses, and trying to the springs. In some places the road is so narrow that when two coaches meet (which was often the case) one of them has to draw up on the bank whilst the other, at the risk of going over, has to pass on the other side (I should have said the opposite side).

We stopped at Dalmally for a fresh relay of horses, when some of the passengers alighted and others scrambled up in their places, till there was not even room for a mouse. And yet if we met a tourist walking on the way the coach was stopped and he was taken up and packed on the luggage which was piled up to any height on the roof. Fortunately the rain ceased and I was able to put down my umbrella and enjoy the most glorious scenery—woods, rocks, rivers, and the beautiful loch Awe and the Pass of Brander.

Mrs Campbell in her wagonette met me where the road turns off to Inverawe. The drive to the house was charming, the most splendid trees I ever saw, and the magnificent River Awe rolling along until it fell into the Loch Ettive about a mile and a half from Inverawe. My dear grandchildren, Sybil and Joyce, greeted me on my arrival. It was about three o'clock and tho' I had had a sleepless night and such a long journey by rail—and such a rough one, 26 miles by coach—I felt as brisk as a bee and ready for anything. But the rain again fell in torrents.

The next day was fine however and Mr Thorpe, a neighbour, invited us to go in his yacht, *The Fern*. We found there several ladies and gentlemen and we all steamed to the very end of Loch Awe where we got out and scrambled up a rock to have luncheon. Table cloths were spread and great preparations for a sumptuous repast—pies and stews and smoking hot potatoes from the yacht. Mr Thorpe gave me what he called

Irish stew but my nose soon found it was not 'savoury meat such as my soul loveth' but what in Scotland is known as 'haggis' and I said to myself, how shall I get rid of it without being so rude as to say it was not eatable, when some wasps came on my plate. So I jumped up crying out, 'Oh! Wasps!' and rushed away letting my stew fall to the ground. I was really hungry but had to go without lunch. We then returned the same way in *The Fern* to Port Sanachon, and in the wagonette to Inverawe. I never saw such miserable huts (for they cannot be called cottages); no chimneys, the smoke coming out where best it might. The women, so ugly, dirty and ragged and the children with no shoes or stockings and their hair all matted together. The women seemed to do the men's work in the fields. I saw them loading hay on a rick etc. (Farming seemed at a very low ebb for oats remained cut for weeks together, uncarried, to the great joy of the crows which helped themselves to any quantity of grain undisturbed. So if I was a crow I should like to be a Scotch one.)

Mrs Campbell was the kindest and most delightful hostess, for she was always contriving some new and pleasant expedition, never sparing her own horses or her purse. As I wished her good night one evening, she said, 'If you don't mind breakfasting at five o'clock tomorrow morning we will drive to Oban to see the Highland Games.'

I replied, 'Oh! I will get up and be enchanted.' Accordingly on Monday morning we had breakfast at five to the minute, and though it poured with rain, we (including Sybil, Joyce and Hunt) ventured in the wagonette—wrapping ourselves in water proof cloaks and hoods, and deluding ourselves into the belief that it would clear up as the day advanced. But no, on the contrary, it never ceased raining, and every now and then came such a heavy pelting fall of rain that it made one's face sore, and wet one's very bones. To hold an umbrella was impossible, for the wind blew a perfect hurricane.

When we arrived at the Great Western Hotel in Oban we were like drowned rats, wet to the skin. We dressed in the hotel and then went to the ground, about a mile from Oban, where the Games were held. It was a most picturesque spot, a beautiful grass sloping meadow, with rocks on all sides, whereon the multitude were seated and standing as thick as a swarm of bees. I was lucky in getting a seat close to a raised wooden platform where the dancing was to take place.

The Games commenced at twelve o'clock with 'throwing the hammer', a trial of strength. Then 'the tossing the caber', most dangerous, then 'racing and jumping', turning men into horses. Then, oh my poor ears! The 'Bagpipes'. Piper after piper, dressed in splendid Highland costume, ascended the platform and marched round and round in the most measured stately way, looking as proud as a peacock and quite as vain as when that beautiful bird struts along with its tail spread open. And the sound that issued from their bagpipes was certainly not more melodious than the peacock's scream before rain.

Then Highland reels: these were so spirited, so joyous; I was delighted. Then followed 'the sword dance', which quite enchanted me. The Princess Louise was to have given away the prizes, but the heavy rain prevented her from coming. Her husband the Marquis of Lorne, however, was present and he assisted Lady Campbell to award them.

We dined at the Great Western Hotel and stayed till after ten o'clock to see the fire works, set up from the yachts. They were beautiful, and the reflection in the water quite lovely. The dear little Sybil and Joyce, who had never seen any before, screamed with delight, and Joyce, when the golden shower from the rockets fell, exclaimed, 'Oh how I wish I could catch some of those sovereigns for Papa!'

It was pitch dark (and we had no lamps) for our drive back, but happily it was fine. We did not get to Inverawe till near one o'clock in the morning.

The 11th was a beautiful day and we had a glorious expedition to Inverary. After an early breakfast we drove to the Pass of Brander where we got into a steamer and crossed Loch Awe at Cladish pier. There we met the Highland coach which was so full of passengers that it seemed impossible to find a seat, and besides ourselves there were many more desiring places. But the coachman, knowing Mrs Campbell, gave the preference to her and her party and managed to stow us all—some inside and some out. I was mounted on the top, squeezed by fat and lean on both sides, and my knees in front so jam'd by other knees that it was most uncomfortable, to say the least of it. The scenery however was so fine that I soon forgot all discomforts.

Inverary Castle is square in form, at the angles are towers. It stands on a spot of great natural beauty. The River Awe runs just beneath the castle, with a lawn of turf like green velvet down to the edge of it. The Princess Louise was at the castle and I wanted Mrs Campbell (as she knew the Princess and the Argyll family) to call there, that I might see the interior of the castle, but she was so shy I could not persuade her. (We saw the Princess driving with the Duke and some of the Ladies Campbell in a barouche with a pair of bays.)

On the last day Mrs Campbell said Sybil and Joyce should have their dinner on the shore and we should all have a grand picnic together. It was immense excitement to the dear grandchildren, gathering sticks to make a fire and boil the potatoes, and make a stew of mutton. In short we were very merry and happy.

About four o'clock I left, as I was getting tired, and walked home. I had just put on my dressing gown, intending to read and rest, when Mrs Campbell appeared and said that she was going in the little open carriage with the ponies to Oban to hear Professor Blackie lecture on the lyric poetry of the Highlands. Would I be up to a 17 miles drive without any dinner, for we must be off directly as it was five o'clock and the lecture began at eight o'clock.

Though I was half dead I replied, 'Oh! I will be up to it.' So I dressed in a trice and away we went and arrived at Oban in good time. In fact, the doors of New Hall were only just opened and we had to wait quite a quarter of an hour before the

Professor, accompanied by the Duke of Argyll, appeared on the platform.

Professor Blackie is a most singular looking man—short, and very slight with long black and scanty locks half way down his back, with a wide brim'd felt hat on his head. His language was eloquent and fluent, the action of his arms was so vehement that I expected every moment he would knock down a garland of laurels which was fastened from pole to pole in front of him. The object of his lecture was the revival of the Gaelic tongue, a language which it was a national disgrace that the Scotchmen should so systematically neglect. He spoke of Ossian and other ancient bards, quoted some of their poetry which he said rivalled Shakespeare, in which opinion I did not agree. The bard Duncan Ban was perhaps the most popular, 'There was a soundness, and a salubrity, a breeziness, a cheerfulness and a genuine mountain flavour about him which could not be too highly valued.' He said much more which made me laugh, for he was too absurd. He stopped in the middle of his lecture and startled us all by saying with his eyes fixed on a lady sitting near me, 'What are you nodding your head about at me?' The poor old soul had the palsy so her head nodded on worse than before. He then repeated his question in a loud and angry tone, so the lady's husband stood up and said his wife was afflicted with the palsy.

It was eleven o'clock before he ended his lecture, and heartily tired I was of him and his Gaelic! He thanked Mrs Campbell for coming, saying he should have miss'd her, 'as he should his front tooth'. It was two o'clock in the morning when we got home, but the drive was charming in the bright moonlight.

September 16th. Alas, my visit ended. Dear kind Mrs Campbell took me to meet the twelve o'clock coach. Had I gone by the eight o'clock I would have had the honour of sitting on the roof with Prince Leopold who went by it to Inverary where the Queen was expected on the following Monday.

When I got back to dear old Charlecote the first thing I did after washing and dressing was to uncover my harp, put on a dozen strings, tune it and play on it till breakfast was ready. After that I went to my dear little cottage, my birds and the garden. I gathered a basketful of roses and arranged all my pretty things in my sitting room (where I am writing this) and in the afternoon drove my pony carriage and felt much refreshed after my long journey. And oh! How I enjoyed my own large bed, the most comfortable of all beds, where I could roll and turn about at my ease and sleep like a top!

Not long after I returned from Scotland, Tina went with her mother to Cannes for the recovery of her health after jaundice, and stayed seven weeks. I must confess I was very happy during her absence, having the full enjoyment of my precious grandchildren, walking and driving in the pony carriage with me and, when their school hours were over, all gathering round in my sitting room for me to amuse them with stories or reading aloud whilst they sat on their little chairs with their knitting or other work. Ada knitted a pair of socks for her Papa. What a pleasure it is to train their young minds in the way they should go.

Soon after Tina's return, Spencer gave a ball and there was a goodly gathering of about 200, but the belles of the ball in my eyes were the four Miss Lucys. They did not make their appearance till about eleven o'clock as they had been put to bed at six to rest and sleep for a few hours to prepare for the coming excitement. When they came into the ball room hand in hand they created quite a sensation and there was a general burst of admiration. They really did look like lovely little fairies. They were dressed with exquisite taste, their frocks were of white tulle all puff'd and flounced over white silk, pink sashes, pink shoes with silk stockings and their frocks being very short their well shaped little legs were shown off to perfection. They had on their heads little wreaths of the most tiny pink roses, with their pretty fair hair hanging down below their waists. Round their necks were gold chains with lockets with diamond crosses. They danced beautifully. I was so delighted watching them that I never once felt tired and at five o'clock in the morning danced the merry and popular 'Sir Roger de Coverley' with as much spirit as though I had been in my teens, instead of the wrong side of seventy.

Well! All things must have an end, so had this ball, which certainly was a decided success for everybody old and young seemed to enjoy it: the music (a band from Birmingham) was first rate, the oak floor perfection for the dances, and the supper pronounced excellent.

The Journals Close

On April 29th, 1876, I went to Droitwich, the oldest and dirtiest and dullest little town in all England! But famous for salt, and its brine baths most efficacious in the cure of rheumatism, gout and neuralgia. My object in going there was to pickle and so cure my thumb which for ten years, ever since my accident, had more or less pained me. Dear Emily Fitzhugh, who suffered much from rheumatism, promised to meet me there.

A nice sort of housekeeper met me and showed me into a small clean bedroom on the ground floor, with one window and no view, and dear Emy had the adjoining bedroom. On my asking for our sitting room she replied we could not have one, everybody had their meals together in one large room and were expected to sit together of an evening in one drawing room, which I in vain protested against.

Presently the doctor came to see me, a kind old man of three score years or more, six foot two, lean as a lizard—quite a Dr Syntax—very courteous manners, and full of the wonderful power and beneficial effects of the brine baths. He ordered me to have a bath at once, but when I got in I pop'd up like a cork and was obliged to have a piece of wood put across to keep me down, as well as Gates to hold me forcibly down by my shoulders. The temperature 95, I was glad when 20 minutes had expired and I was allowed to get out.

At two o'clock a bell rang for luncheon and we went into a very large room with a long table, a very dirty table cloth with very little food on it, and 16 rheumatic, neuralgic and gouty patients sitting round it, and some horrible looking stew at the top. I looked at it in despair for I was very hungry after my journey and my bath. I picked and pecked at a bit of the mutton and finally left it on the plate.

In the evening the doctor, according to his custom, went the round of all his patients to administer a dose of rhubarb. He came to me first and, with a bottle in his hand, asked Gates for a wine glass into which he put some rhubarb out of his bottle, mix'd it with water, and then, bringing it to me, said, 'Now Mrs Lucy, you will be so good as to open your mouth wide and swallow this. It is not at all bad, and you shall have a goody,' shaking a fruit lozenge from another bottle he took out of his pocket. Oh! It was horrible and tortured my poor stomach all night. Dear Emy had to undergo the same treatment and with the same result.

Breakfast at nine o'clock and a very bad one, the bread heavy as lead, dry toast not half toasted and thick enough for a plough boy, fat bacon ill cured, no hen eggs, but ducks' that I fancied might not be fresh. At eleven o'clock we had our brine bath, and I did not dislike it quite as much.

Sir Thomas and Lady Riddle arrived that evening, he seemed a martyr to gout and had tried the brine baths before. Lady Riddle was a great acquisition for she sang, and tho' her voice was on the wane, she had been well taught and pronounced her words so clear, which to me is always a charm. A Mr Bailey, an old college friend of my brother William, was amongst some fresh arrivals. He had a black servant, an Arab, who had become a Christian and was god son to his master. Then there was Mr Ridley, brother to the late Sir Mathew Ridley who I used to know so well. He was always dressed in an entire suit of black velvet, and wore his hat at breakfast. And there was Mrs Baring of Norman Court, a fine lady, a perfect cripple, wearing a marvellous cap and her black hair all flying and frizzy. Poor soul! I thought that no amount of pickling could set her on her legs again.

While we were there, Emily and I one day drove along the Stoke road and passed Mr Corbett MP's new residence, an immense pile of building of brick and stone, like a French chateau with the most elaborate iron entrance gates with the arms and crest on every part where it was possible to put them. The salt town of Stoke is the property of Mr Corbett and all its inhabitants are employed in the salt works, on which he has expended half a million of money. He has built nice cottages with gardens for the work people, schools for boys and girls, with a house for the master, and pays the stipend of a clergy-man of the Church of England to minister their spiritual wants etc. What a blessing it would be if there were more capitalists of the stamp of this worthy Mr Corbett!

May 23rd, oh, joy of joy! was our last day at the Royal Brine Baths. I never was more weary of any place, but I must say my thumbs were considerably better, but I fear dear Emily's rheumatism was not cured. I arrived at dear Charlecote about seven o'clock and did I not enjoy the good tender mutton at dinner, and roll about, without the fear of falling, in my own comfortable large bed!

On Palm Sunday [1879] I was taken ill of bronchitis and the doctor was sent for. He ordered me to bed and said I had bronchial asthma. I was covered with mustard and linseed poultices and he desired Gates to give me whisky toddy. For a week I suffered severely for want of breath and a terrible cough. Gates's good nursing, with God's blessing, I am sure greatly aided my recovery, for she never spared herself by night as well as day. She was always ready with a poultice, Bow's Liniment or Ray's Essence of Linseed, and then 'the whisky toddy' which Dr Mackee insisted on my taking as often as I could. There never was an invalid better cared for.

Dear Emily came to see me and the next day Mr Thomas came and staid till the 21st. He told me he was engaged to be married to Alice Reute, a pupil of his, who was very clever and played very well on the piano and harp. They were to be married the following week. I was still too poorly to touch my harp, but I dined downstairs as it was dear Ada's thirteenth birthday and, as the 315th of Shakespeare's, marked the opening of the Shakespeare Memorial Theatre at Stratford-on-Avon. Many noted actors came down from London for the week to act some of his plays. The weather was bitterly cold and wet so I was unable to attend till the last evening, when we all went to the comedy of 'As You Like It', one of my favourite plays of Shakespeare. My dear grandchildren were wild with delight when in Act Two Scene One, the Forest of Arden, a Charlecote deer (which their Papa, as requested, had shot for the occasion) appeared on the stage, and Masters, the Charlecote keeper dressed up as a forester, led on two of the deer hounds. The effect was charming and the house rang with shouts of applause and encore. We all came home saying we had never enjoyed a play so much before.

August 4th. Spencer, Tina and I went to Ragley to meet the Princess Mary Duchess of Teck and the Duke her husband. A meeting of the Alcester Labourers Improvement Society (of which Lord Hertford is the founder and president) is annually held in the park and prizes are given by their kind landlord for good conduct, neatness in their houses etc.; and there the cottagers display their vegetables, flowers, and also their work such as knitting, sewing etc. The Princess Mary distributed the prizes.

It was a glorious afternoon happily, for as yet we had had no summer, the weather nothing but cold, rain and thunder storms. Everybody seemed to enjoy themselves, for the princess by the courtesy of her own unaffected hilarity diffused ease and pleasure all around. Nothing was chilled by ceremonial, or etiquette. The Duke of Teck has agreeable manners, a fine figure and a handsome face. The Duchess is said to be the largest woman in the Kingdom.

I went in my brougham with Cock Robin and Fire Fly who

took me the 14 miles in an hour and 50 minutes. Spencer and Tina followed in their barouche. When I got to the house the footman said Lady Hertford, the Princess and all the lords and ladies had just gone—some in carriages and some on foot—to the tent in the park, and Lady Hertford had left orders for the coming guests to follow. So Fred drove me through a dense crowd of people to the tent, where I alighted and was immediately introduced by kind Lord Hertford to Her Royal Highness and the Duke who both shook hands with me and enquired if I had had far to drive etc.

Tea, coffee and fruit etc. were laid out on tables under the large portico for the Princess, Duke of Teck and the grandees; whilst we, the smaller fry, had the same in the dinner room. After I had had a cup of coffee I went with Lady Ernest Seymour into the flower garden which Lady Hertford has created and laid out with the most perfect taste. When we returned to the house Lady Hertford met me and said, 'My dear Mrs Lucy, where have you been? I have been looking for you so! I want you to come and talk to Princess Mary.' And away she took me to the portico, and seated me on a chair beside her Royal Highness who was busy eating strawberries and cream, but not too busy to exclaim, 'Look! Look! Mrs Lucy, my gown! My beautiful gown! Alas!' and I saw that a swallow (for there were many nests under the pillars) had muted on it, so I took my pocket handkerchief and wiped it off and said, 'How fortunate you were not looking up or you might have had it in your eye and been blinded like Tobit was,' which amused her very much and she laughed heartily.

When she had eaten her strawberries, I was going to take her plate away but she held it fast and, like a child, cried out, 'Oh, I have not finished!' There was some of the cream still on the plate, which she spooned into her mouth; then I got her a fresh plate full and, taking off the stalks of the strawberries, mashed them with lots of cream and sugar, and she was so pleased, gave me one of her sweetest smiles and soon cleared that plate. She has an immense appetite for everything, as well as fruit. I found her most agreeable and, after speaking very graciously about various things, she said, 'Now tell me about Charlecote.' I then told her that I lived there with my son and his wife and that I had four dear little grand daughters. 'What, no boy!' she exclaimed. 'You must have a grandson! I have three boys and one girl. I wish we could change for I love girls best, tho' my little sons are considered very handsome.' She then desired me to bring Spencer and Tina to introduce to her, which of course I gladly did.

That summer was followed by a severe winter. The Avon rose to such a height, covering the marble vases on the lower steps of the terrace. Spencer lost all his meadow hay to the value of £700. The previous year too all the hay in the place meadow was carried away by a flood and for the last three years the harvest had been so bad that farmers were unable to pay their rent and many had thrown up their farms: Spencer had five in Hampton Lucy parish on his hands. Many of his tenants were asking for a reduction of rent, which he was obliged to grant for fear of having more farms on his hands. The times for agriculturalists are too sad! Spencer's income was reduced more than half.

Yet how happily the New Year's Morning of 1880 began. The bell once again rang for family prayer and I had the joy of seeing Spencer, his wife and children, and all the household assembled in the Great Hall to pray together. From the time I was married we always had family prayer morning and night and so it continued for some years after Spencer's marriage, and then to my great sorrow was discontinued.

In August Mrs John Thomas gave birth to a son. I was asked to be one of its godmothers. Mrs Thomas had a very good confinement and no drawback for the first six weeks, but then I received a letter from Mr Thomas saying, 'I am sure you will feel with me when I tell you that Alice has been dangerously ill since Saturday, suffering most agonising pains from internal cold and inflammation, the result of a very short walk with me on Friday last. She has had Dr Murray who attended her during her confinement. He has been here twice a day ever since. Yesterday morning he pronounced her in danger but today we hope there is an improvement for the better. I am sure she would join me in best love if she were well enough to be spoken to.' Two days after, she breathed her last. Poor dear Mr Thomas, it was all so sudden it was well nigh his own death stroke, they were so devoted to each other. She was only 25 years of age.

After the funeral we persuaded him to come to us at Christmas, promising that he should be as quiet as he liked and find no one but ourselves, his oldest friends. He spent his evenings with me in my sitting room and it was a great comfort to him to pour out his grief to me who so deeply sympathised with him, and at the end of a fortnight when he returned to London he was calmer and more resigned.

On the 29th of June, 1881, I went to London for Lord Brooke's marriage to Miss Maynard. The wedding was to take place in Westminster Abbey with full choral service. I hired a nice brougham and started at half past two o'clock for the Abbey. When I arrived the nave was densely filled and the whole of the Abbey was thronged with spectactors, but a broad pathway was railed off for the invited guests and for the bridal procession so that not the slightest inconvenience was occasioned by the throng. I got a capital seat by the Chandos Leighs in a front row near the altar. The Prince and Princess of Wales, Princess Louise Marchioness of Lorne, the Duke and Duchess of Connaught, Princess Mary Duchess of Teck and their several lords and ladies in attendance, came in as the clock struck the half hour past three, and soon after Lord Brooke with Prince Leopold, his best man, arrived.

The organ then pealed forth with its richest tones the march and chorus 'Twine ye the Garlands' and the bride came leaning on Lord Rosslyn's arm, looking 'simple perfection' in an exquisite dress of white satin duchess lace and fringes of orange flowers. She carried a great bouquet of Marechal Niel roses. She was followed by twelve bride's maids, and each wore a spray of daisies in pearls and diamonds, the gift of the bridegroom, a pretty design and a pretty compliment to his bride, as she was called from her childhood by the pet name of Daisy. The Bishop of St Albans, assisted by the other Divines, solemnised part of the marriage ceremony (which I do not like or approve).

The sight in the fine old Abbey was truly grand and one not easily to be forgotten. Alwyn Greville took me through the crowd, got me a wedding favour and put me into my brougham and I was soon at 7 Carlton Gardens, as I had been invited to the breakfast where the Royal Family and all the most distinguished people were assembled.

Alwyn took me to the library to see the wedding presents which were display'd on long tables covered with crimson cloth. First there was china, countless beautiful tea services etc. etc., then plate—gold and silver—then jewellery; the most dazzling costly array: the inhabitants of Warwick gave a diamond necklace which I admired greatly, tho' composed of small stones; the Prince and Princess of Wales, a splendid bracelet of diamonds and sapphires. Amongst the smaller gifts Spencer's and Tina's was as pretty as any, a gold band bracelet with carbuncles and diamond stars. Then there was a quantity of rare articles of vertu. In short there was more than enough of precious things to confuse the eye and defy description but before I had seen half of these rare and costly gifts the groom of the chambers asked me if I would not like to go upstairs for refreshments. Why he singled me out of the many who were hovering round the tables looking at the presents, I could not guess.

He ushered me into the large drawing room where there was one round table with the immense wedding cake in the middle of it, and all sorts of delicacies, especially for the Royal party; and there were a few small tables besides, at one of which I seated myself with the said groom of the chambers, a most gentlemanlike man who was most polite—asking me what I should like, etc. Dear Lady Warwick soon joined me and we talked over the happy events of the day. Lord and Lady Rosslyn were most cordial and seeing Lord Brooke at the other end of the room with the Baroness Burdett Coutts I went and wished him every possible happiness. When the Baroness shook hands with me I said, 'You must allow me to take this opportunity of wishing you all the happiness this world can bestow' (for she had only recently become a bride), on which she gave me a most gracious smile and her thanks, evidently pleased, but turning her head she muttered, 'Few have wished me happiness!'

Lord Brooke then left us and she introduced me to her young husband, who I thought looked like an attorney's clerk. She spoke of Charlecote and how she admired it and hoped some day she might be permitted to show it to Mr Bartlett etc. She asked if I ever went to the play. I replied, 'Oh yes, I enjoy a play very much if it is a good one.' So she took her ivory out of her pocket and said, 'Will you have my box at the Lyceum for this evening?' I thanked her accordingly and put the token into my pocket. It was now six o'clock and we all adjourned downstairs to see the bride off.

Coming out of the library Princess Mary Duchess of Teck recognised me and greeted me most warmly, and after a little chat went up to the Princess of Wales, who with the Princess Louise was standing not far off, and said to her, 'You must let me introduce Mrs Lucy to you,' on which the Princess, with her sweet smile, and charming manners, advanced and shook me by the hand. I was so astonished and felt so honoured that I thought some fairy had turned *me* into an old princess!

The Duchess of Teck afterwards said to me, 'I thought it would give you pleasure to be introduced to the Princess of Wales!' 'Indeed it did,' I replied, 'and how good and kind of you to do me such an honour!' Soon after this Lord Rosslyn appeared with the bride in her travelling dress. The carriage was at the door to take them to the station, the twelve bride's maids were prepared with satin shoes and an abundance of rice. 'But where is the bridegroom!' Lord Rosslyn shouted. 'Brooke! Brooke! Where are you? The carriage waits. You will miss the train!' Then turning to Lord Warwick who was standing by me, he said, 'Perhaps the father will do as well. Come along, Warwick,' making the dear Lord who is so shy blush to his ears. However, the true bridegroom came rushing down the stairs and, with a chorus of our united good wishes, old shoes flying and rice showering, Lord and Lady Brooke stepped into the carriage and were off. God bless them! I do think there never could be a more perfect couple, or a more splendid and perfect wedding.

The Princess of Wales' carriage was then announced but there was no Miss Knollys, so the Princess drove off without her. Poor Miss Knollys came breathless and was in despair when she found she was too late. Princess Louise then went, taking no notice of Miss Knollys' distress, but the good natured Princess Mary said, 'Come, I will take you.' My own brougham came directly and away I was driven to Welbeck Street where I was staying. I bid the coachman come again at 7.30 to take me to the Lyceum, and invited Miss Stone to go with me. I dressed with all speed, and just as I sat down to dinner the brougham was at the door, so, with a morsel of chicken in my mouth, I jumped into the carriage and with Miss Stone got to the theatre as the first act of 'The Cup' had commenced. It is a tragedy by Tennyson in two acts, and I delighted in sitting at my ease in the baroness's comfortable arm chair, retiring every now and again from the glare behind the muslin curtains lined with pale blue satin. Miss Stone amused me by saying that young men were continually passing backwards and forwards trying to peep into the box, which she thought most impertinent; but I laughed and said, 'Very natural, expecting to see the aged bride, of course.'

The next evening I was to dine in Portman Square with Sir Edward and Lady Blackett to meet my brother William and his wife. I ordered a four wheeler as it still rained in torrents, but a hansom at the moment was passing and the servant, instead of fetching a cab, hailed it, and I was obliged to throw the long train of my gown over my shoulders and get into it. When the door bell was rung two tall fine powdered footmen appeared and ushered me into a splendid drawing room, the walls hung with the most beautiful tapestry I ever saw in this country. The colours were just as fresh as though it had been just done, whereas it was more than a hundred years old, the possessor having been the Duke of Gloucester, brother of George III, for whom the house had been purchased, and decorated by Italian artists. Some of the panels were painted exquisitely, as well as the ceiling.

Lady Blackett is 40 years younger than Sir Edward, who has already had three if not four wives, and the curious thing is that when she first came out she was engaged to Sir Edward Blackett's eldest son, who *jilted* her. She is sister to my brother Willy's wife. Sir Edward is a regular made-up old dandy, with a wig, false dyed moustache, false teeth and very crochety on his legs! But what does that matter? When a man, however old, has a fine house in the country, ditto in London and a fine income, he can always get a wife, and I am sorry to say a young one too if he wishes it. A rich old woman also can get a penniless young man for her husband, for instance the poor Baroness Cheque Book, as an American named the Baroness Burdett Coutts.

In January 1883 I had a terrible fall down stairs. The housemaid had taken up the stair carpet and, like a thoughtless and foolish woman, had been beeswaxing the oak steps so that they were as slippery as glass. I, with my large watch in my hand, coming out of my bedroom, was going to my sitting room, and no sooner had I got to the top of the stairs than my feet slipped from under me and I and my watch rolled down together. My wretched back was bumped and bumped on the edge of each step till I fairly believed it must be broken, and I groaned and almost howled like a dog at the moon before I could get up. I did not send for the doctor but doctored myself with lots of leeches, many poultices and other disagreeable remedies.

March 7th, a few weeks after my fall, was Sybil's birthday. She invited every child in the neighbourhood to tea and games, making 28 children. It was quite a pretty sight to see all their happy faces round the table in the large dinner room. The day was unfortunately so cold with heavy snow storms that they could not play out of doors, but did they scamper all over the house: upstairs and downstairs and in my lady's chamber! I had still not recuperated from my fall and must confess I was *not* sorry when I heard the sound of the last carriage wheels rolling away. But as I lay in my room, hearing from my window the happy squeals of Sybil's departing playmates, I was forcibly struck by the accelerating speed with which the thread of life unravels. My dear Ada was now seventeen, the age when young ladies came out and were marriageable. Yet I hoped dear Ada would enjoy life unfettered for some years. 'Think of living!! Thy life is no idle dream, but a solemn reality, it is thy own; it is all thou hast to front eternity with' (Carlyle).

I had always said that if I was alive and well when Ada went to her first ball, I would give her her ball dress and go and see her dance; and so it came to pass and I attended at the age of 80 the Warwick Hunt Ball. The Warwicks most kindly asked me to stay at the Castle as it would be much less fatiguing going to the ball from there than driving to and fro from Charlecote.

I arrived in the ball room about 10.30, some little time before the Charlecote party, and Lady Warwick and I struggled through the assembled crowd to the top of the room and secured seats. I was anxiously looking out for Ada to make her appearance, and when she did come I thought how nice she looked in her simple and elegant dress of pure white, the skirt clouds of tulle, the body satin, and a wreath of snowdrops from the shoulder along half the front (the present fashion). Her necklace and bracelets of Roman pearls were the gift of her Uncle Berkeley Lucy and her pretty fan of white feathers, a present from her aunt. As I watched her dancing, all the happy memories of my own first ball floated before me! And at the same time reminded me most forcibly of the loss of youth! Still I will say in spite of my four score years I enjoyed myself thoroughly, seeing how much my dearly loved Ada was enjoying *herself*. And then it was a pleasure meeting so many of my old friends, all greeting me so warmly and telling me how young and well I was looking. 'Fine feathers make fine birds' and so a fine brocaded black satin dress with beautiful diamonds can make even a grand mother look well, and Gates had done her best to set me off to the best advantage. But no flattery could make me forget 'what manner of woman I am!' though dear shy Lord Warwick kindled a little spark of dormant vanity in me when he exclaimed, 'Mrs Lucy, I do admire you! You are beautifully dressed as a lady ought to be, and as I like to see her!'

Lord Yarmouth took me to supper, there was every delicacy to invite an appetite, but I never care to eat at twelve o'clock at night. At 1.30 Lady Warwick and I came away in my little brougham, having left the rest of the party to dance till four o'clock in the morning. It was a very full ball, too crowded for the display of fine steps. Lady Warwick, as we wished each other good night, said, 'Breakfast will be at 9.30, but dear Mrs Lucy, don't think of coming down, have yours in bed, as I shall.'

'Oh no,' I replied, 'I shall be down all right,' and I was; to the minute, a full hour before anyone appeared, excepting Lord Warwick who had gone only briefly to the ball. So he and I breakfasted *tête à tête*. I was astonished at myself not feeling the least tired.

On Monday the 21st Lord Hertford was thrown from his horse in the hunting field, and the greatest anxiety was felt by everyone about him. The Warwickshire Hounds had met at Ragley; the meet was a large one and the day fine. A start was made across the Park, and coverts were drawn blank till at last a fox was found. At this time Lord Hertford was in a meadow adjoining the wood. He was riding a horse he had recently purchased from Lord Willoughby de Broke.* Mr Harrison saw him galloping across the meadow and very shortly afterwards Mr Harrison observed about halfway across the meadow a horse and a gentleman lying on the ground—to all appearance both dead. He immediately dismounted and raised the head and, to his grief and horror, saw that the man was Lord Hertford. He was lying on his chest and his head close to the horse's loins and his foot in the stirrup. He was quite unconscious and bleeding from the mouth and nose. It is supposed that the horse must have had heart disease which caused it to fall, as the ground was perfectly level. It fell on its head and rolled over on its side, legs uppermost, crushing poor dear Lord Hertford by its weight.

Drs Forbes and Hobbs who were both out hunting were quickly on the spot. A bed was got from the nearest cottage, placed on a gate and Lord Hertford, laid thereupon, was carried by several gentleman to Ragley. The journey took two hours. On arriving, whilst being taken up the stone steps, he opened his eyes and faintly murmured 'no more'.

Dr Denning was telegraphed for from London and was at Ragley that evening, but no human skill could avail, his injuries were fatal. The spine was broken, four ribs too, and the chest injured and his limbs paralysed. The greatest sympathy was evinced, and 300 telegrams were received on the following day—the Queen and every member of the Royal Family telegraphing daily expressing their deepest sympathy and asking for information etc. He could take no nourishment and was only semi-conscious at times.

On Thursday his brain seemed clearer and he recognised all the members of his family and spoke in his usual bright and cheerful manner, but about noon a relapse occurred. By Friday the whole of his body was paralysed and at half past seven o'clock that evening what remained of life became extinct.

*The Barnard nephew who had inherited.

The loss of a life so endeared to all about him, and so valued by a host of friends, can hardly be measured in the first moment of bereavement. Adored by his family, loved, esteemed and admired by all who had ever come in contact with him, from his sovereign the Queen to his humblest neighbour, Lord Hertford's memory will long live among all who respect a noble character. He was a man of the highest principles, kind and courteous, endowed with a winning charm of manner, beloved in his County and looked upon there as a model not only of the most high bred and perfect gentleman, but one always willing to give his valuable services to promote any benevolent or charitable object. He was buried on the 31st, the weather was cold and wretched, a drizzling rain falling the whole day, which contributed to the gloom which prevailed. The funeral was attended by thousands of all ranks, special trains on the Great Western and Midland Railways brought large numbers of personal friends and relatives, and representatives of all the Royal Family.

In accordance with the wishes of the family the funeral was conducted in a very unostentatious manner: no hearse with its waving black plumes of feathers, no dismal mourning coaches, no scarfs or hat bands; and though the weather was terrible everyone walked on foot. The procession, numbering at least 500, started from Ragley at 2.30 and at the entrance gates (quite a mile from the Hall) was joined by the various deputations from public bodies. The route was thronged by thousands, despite the downpour of rain, all the way to the little church at Arrow; and there numbers of county gentlemen and friends were congregated to pay their last tribute of respect to the lamented Marquis.

July 1883. It is now nearly twelve months since I first took up my pen to write this sketchy autobiography and time seems never to have impaired my memory (frequently a painful one) for my whole life, with all its days, has been present to me like a picture which cannot be effaced, whose colours never grow faint, and many a tear has drop'd from my eyes whilst recording past sorrows which it pleased God to afflict me with.

I have just returned from Plas Power and there I walked with dear Emily through the wood to the bridge, at the very end resting on a camp stool. I fear I shall not be up to such a walk again, it used to be my favourite one which I never missed taking, but old age now creeps on apace and I cannot expect to do as I was wont. I am 80 years of age. Oh how can I reckon up this mighty number of years without thanking the Almighty for having guided me so far under His protection! And for wonderful health, very few grey hairs and sound teeth. To be so old and to feel at the same time young and susceptible of all the enjoyments of life is tantalising—to see oneself in a looking glass and think how strange it is that housed within is still that young Welsh girl. And looking back, to see how things come and go in a continuous stream, our joys and sorrows, our hopes and fears, and all the incidents and accidents of life—and how things pass!

The last volume of the journals is unfinished and is rather unfocused, a series of diary entries. Visitors to Charlecote come and go. Weather begins to be more and more important to the writer of the journals, whose winter attacks of bronchitis had become chronic and whose girth—she really was large by now, like the Queen—rendered her breathless at the least exertion. More and more she was confined to her 'dear snug little room' by frost (slippery paths), snow, and the damp fogs that disabled her rheumatic hands from sweeping the strings of her harp. But the rain had to be heavy to prevent her going out in her pony chaise behind May Fly or Cock Robin to cheer up her now very old sister, Emma Williams, who had a house at Wasperton up the river, or to take cake and pineapples to Berkeley's children at Holly Lodge in the next village. Neighbours brought their friends to hear her play duets with her granddaughters and with Mr Thomas. (Not many elderly ladies have a tame harpist at their beck and call, and the Queen's Official Harpist at that, for this Mr Thomas now was.)

Mr Thomas came for Easter week and brought his dear little boy, a fine intelligent child and very clever at figures. His great delight is in calculation and you can hardly puzzle him if you ask him to add up any number however large. He is himself in perpetual motion and the first day when he arrived and came into this room with his father to see me he was like a young bull in a china shop, rushing about and seizing hold of everything, and jumping from chair to chair; putting me in a fright for all my pretty things and making me cry out, 'Oh! You must not touch that!' and Mr Thomas in vain telling him to sit still. He coolly said to his father, 'Why did you come here? Let us go home, I don't want to stay here!' Such a pity he has been so spoiled, no doubt by Miss Stone who has had the sole management of him since his poor mother's death. But we all now try to impress on Mr Thomas the importance of correcting him etc.

July 1887. Intense heat, it withers all my bright ideas, and it is absurd to write down the same daily routine of going out in the pony chaise. Spencer's hay and clover in Charlecote parish will be all carried by tomorrow and got without a drop of rain, such a thing has never happened before in my memory. The grass was cut one day and made the next.

January 27th, 1888. Spencer dined and slept at Kineton, Lord Willoughby invited him, the meet being at Farnborough. So sad! Owing to these terrible times of poverty for country gentlemen (having farms on their hands and getting such reduced rents for those which are tenanted) Lord Willoughby has let Compton to a rich Mr Cassel, a German, and now lives in a small house in Kineton. Spencer returned full of a most laughable incident. Mr Cassel [*later Sir Ernest Cassel*] had some German friends to shoot. The keeper (Creed) who had been many years keeper at Compton shouted, 'Bear to the left' (the birds flying to the left), when one of the Germans threw down his gun and in mortal fright climbed up the nearest tree thinking the keeper had seen a bear approaching!

January 28th, 1888. George Granville (from Wellesbourne) dined here and after nine o'clock we were all anxiously looking out for the total eclipse of the moon. I came up to my dear little boudoir and seated myself at the south window, and gazed in silence at the beautiful and soul-stirring sight. It was a dark night sky, clear and cloudless, besprinkled with stars, the air cold and frosty—and my poor understanding was quite unable to grasp the marvellous accuracy which the science of astronomy has reached, for at 9.30 p.m., exactly as predicted, the first contact of the moon with the earth's shadow began, and at 10.31 p.m. the moon was wholly plunged into the earth's shadow—and then I plunged under the bedclothes!

She rose above her ailments with a spurt of her youthful resilience, taking her maid Gates up to London with her in order that she might consult a specialist about a small cyst on her chin. She insisted that the operation to remove it be carried out immediately in her hotel bedroom, with Gates hovering in terror with towels and hot water. She was given chloroform (the Queen had been given it when in labour. Mary Elizabeth had gone through her childbirths without anything, and was curious to test its effect). On coming round she demanded to be shown the offending object which turned out to be the size of a Fortnum and Mason dried cherry. She was vain enough to be pleased that the cut left no scar.

But her curiosity was slackening, like her own élan vital. *'I could not undertake another long journey,' she wrote, 'for, as Walter Scott when he was growing old said of himself, "I am getting very unlocomotive—something like an old cabinet that looks well enough in its own corner but will scarce bear wheeling about even to be dusted."' She was beginning to worry, as she had not done before, about Spencer's unlet farms, about the girls' futures, about the servants' overdue wages.*

The girls had plenty of parties, tennis was superseding croquet; they had a new boat for river picnics and were photographed in it in smart straw 'boaters', strumming banjos. The masculine fashion of hard hats, collars and ties, did not become them; their grandmother was worried about them. They were such dear good girls, deserving of the best of men. Yet in the end Ada and Linda would have to fall back on marriages with husbands younger than themselves, marriages which Mary Elizabeth would have done her utmost to prevent.

Her closest friend, as with most elderly Victorian ladies, was her maid, Gates, who knew her more intimately than anyone and who alternately scolded and petted her. Beneath the tester of a bed upholstered in amber silk brocade (which she and George had bought for a guinea a yard in 1830) veiled with white Swiss, she sat propped by frilled pillows, her occupations strewn over the ample surface. Piled on the bedside table would be the devotional books bound in limp calf without which no one of her age could sleep, her passport to Eternity—from 'Stepping Heavenward' to Thomas à Kempis.

The Doctor advised her to get up in the night when she could not breathe and walk about or sit for half an hour in an armchair—'so I have had the old-fashioned high-backed armchair in which old Mr Lucy [her father-in-law, the Reverend John Lucy] 65 years ago breathed his last, brought into my bedroom. I get up and sit in the old chair and commune with my own heart and feel I am alone with God.'

Tuesday May 22nd 1888. Very cold N.E. wind. Bawbee and Corsair with Arthur (coachman) and groom went to London for Spencer and Ada to ride. [*They had taken a house in Portland Place for the season.*] Dear Spencer went to London to join his wife and girls. He was very loath to leave me, and I was to part with him, and shall miss him dreadfully in the evening. I am not well enough to play my dear harp but must beguile by the spell of fiction the tedious hours between my dinner at seven and bedtime at ten.

She changed her diet, went on to brandy instead of whisky, eschewed cauliflower and all vegetables but asparagus, but without much effect.

One of her goldfinches died. Charlecote was intolerably lonely without young company. She decided to join her family in Portland Place, which she forthwith did and her breathlessness and sleeplessness improved. Company was always a tonic to her and she plunged (her favourite word and an apt one) with gusto into all the entertainments offered. The June of 1888 was cold and wet but so improved were her spirits that she was not prevented by it from visiting and enjoying visitors, mostly country neighbours up for the Season. She husbanded her strength for a promised treat, a harp concert by Mr Thomas in St James's Hall, for which he had sent them all tickets.

It was indeed a *grand* concert in every sense of the word. Mr Thomas outdid himself in his exquisite playing of a most difficult and beautiful Fantasia 'Sounds of Ossian' . . . The band of harps, 22 in number, was very good and all the lady harpists being dressed in white had a charming effect. I was so delighted that I never felt tired and stayed till it was over.

Gates accompanied her in a hansom cab to the Royal Academy and to see the Panorama of Niagara:

It is perfectly marvellous and beautiful, the deception is so great that it is almost impossible to believe that you are not standing dangerously near and looking at the very Falls—and that you may not get wet from the spray and foam of the dashing water.

Back to Charlecote, to her caged birds and her snug sitting room; back to the nagging fear that Spencer was overspending on an ever diminishing income, that the household would have to be cut down (only Tina was such a poor manager, how could she do without a housekeeper?), that the girls would have to share a hunter, and that they were no nearer to finding themselves husbands.

*   The last words of the last volume of the journals run down hill as if her hand were growing too weak to hold the pen:*

The New Year has opened with the most gloomy weather, the whole earth is covered with a dense fog and I feel far from well having had sleepless nights, but let me not complain but pray to God to give me more heart.

So she broke off. She fought against becoming bedridden but insisted on getting up and sitting by her bedroom fire in old John Lucy's wing armchair. The girls paid her short visits, timed so as not to tire her, and Tina, who had a sweet low voice, read prayers to her. There were to be no more musical evenings.

Spencer, who had always been able to cheer and amuse her with his stable yard imitations, could not make her smile—she was already in the way to study a long silence.

Her last attack of bronchitis came in February 1889. She was carried on a farm cart behind her pony Cock Robin along the church avenue through thin winter sunshine to the churchyard, not to lie among the other sleepers in that quiet earth as she had once hoped to do, and have her children plant roses over her and water her grave with their tears, but in the vault of the church which she had built.

AFTERWARDS

Afterwards

The room in which she penned those last words is just as she left it, only now the crimson brocade curtains are threadbare and the harp strings broken. Family history is written in shredding silk, peeling wallpaper, worn-out toys, carriage harness, school books. In fading watercolours her children are eternally fixed in their innocence with hobby horse and parrot. One of William Fulke's childish frocks has been lovingly preserved—perhaps the dress he was wearing when the Princess Victoria hugged him in Kensington Gardens. And still carefully packed in a chest of drawers is the tiny, exquisitely appliqué'd satin dress in which Mary Elizabeth was married.

In this room, too, Mary Elizabeth as an old woman looked fondly on the four little granddaughters who would spend their lives in another century. The granddaughters had been her solace; they were gentle and biddable, submitting to being taught the harp by Mr Thomas and Latin by a strict Russian governess. Neither of these accomplishments was going to be of the slightest use to them in later life. As children they were cocooned in the safest of all safe worlds—that of the English landed gentry, with no experiences more upsetting than the loss of a pet or the daily disagreeableness of being strapped to a back-board in order that their backs might grow straight. The routine of their days was pleasantly the same:

prayers before breakfast, harp and piano practice in the morning, drives in the pony carriage with their mother in the afternoon to call on newcomers to the neighbourhood, reading and studying before tea, music in the library after dinner, then more prayers before bedtime. Until they were in their teens all four girls slept in the nursery, with its coloured prints of Miss Muffet and Gainsborough's 'Blue Boy', and its dapple-grey rocking horse with scarlet nostrils; a childhood from the stories of Mrs Molesworth and Mrs Ewing, and the comfortable world of the nineteenth-century landed classes.

Only with hindsight does it become apparent that the meridian of the Victorian high summer was already passed. Mary Elizabeth could not have perceived it, believing as she did implicitly in Providence, Queen and Empire. But there were signs for those who could interpret them, infallible as the shepherd's warning about the streaks of red on the horizon across the river in the early morning.

Henry Spencer was the last Lucy to enjoy his inheritance. Behind him was the English squirearchy, generations of it stretching back, his justification for the only sort of life he knew how to live. When unpaid bills mounted he sold George Lucy's collection of paintings piecemeal. (The houses in London, taken in order to give the girls a chance to find husbands, the hunters, the shooting parties, the grouse moors in Scotland—all these were looked on as necessities; old masters were expendable.) Only a few months after his mother's death, Spencer succumbed to pneumonia from getting wet through while out shooting—he who had been in his lifetime one of the finest shots in England, and in all weathers. A contemporary described him as 'first-rate company, with a ready laugh and a philosophy quaint and attractive from its apparently rustic derivation but tinctured with a great deal more common sense than is possessed by some who possibly know their Plato better than he'.

Spencer had hoped for a son-in-law who would carry Charlecote on in the tradition he himself had inaugurated. His

mother had said to him more than once that she was growing
uneasy about Ada. The Warwicks' charming sons had found
wives (heiresses), the eldest Hertford boy had stayed frequently at Charlecote but showed no sign of being attracted by
any of the Lucy daughters (much preferring their amusing
grandmother). Yet invitations that included duck shooting
or a day out with the Warwicks were never refused. Spencer
was generous about providing horses and was a delightful host,
full of entertaining stories and imitations. Charlecote, warmed
now by hot air through ornamental grills in the floors, was
such a pleasant house to come back to, with a prospect of roast
venison and '57 claret, that young men were ready to make
themselves agreeable and even to listen to harp duets in the
library after dinner. But to no purpose. The two elder girls did
not marry young, their grandmother never had the joy of
seeing her own lace wedding veil setting off 'a marriage
morning face'. In photographs, Ada, even in girlhood, looks
careworn, pinched, feeling the strain of being the eldest and
the heir.

Charlecote's happy *vie de château* did not survive Spencer.
Like a needle pointing north steadily, Tina's homing instinct
made her for once decisive. It was explained to her by the
lawyers that the house would have to be let for a term of years
and most of the servants turned off. They dared not sound
optimistic and were alert to check any hopes she might indulge
in of the old wasteful way of life returning. Their caution was
unnecessary; to Tina it was the order of release. Her mind was
made up: she and the girls would live in a rented house until
they should marry and set her free to go back to her own
people.

The poor girls were wretched and wept with the servants,
who felt betrayed by their employers. Tina ordered the agent
to make a bonfire in the court; into it went inventories, letters,
medieval charters, and title deeds spanning four hundred
years. (The five black notebooks from a stationer's in Warwick, containing the journals, lay unnoticed in the drawer into

which they had been tidied away.) For eight years strangers rented the house.

Tina, marrying very young, had been delivered over to a dominating mother-in-law, being expected only to grace her husband's table and to produce sons. Now she rallied determinedly; within three years she hurried Ada into a marriage that would shift the burden of inheritance on to masculine shoulders and took herself and two unmarried daughters to her mother's property in Inverness-shire on the shores of Loch Leven, there to have a late blooming. But it was not until she became an elderly lady of some local standing in the Highlands that she regained the regal carriage and confidence that had made her such a stunner at nineteen.

Ada married in 1892 Henry Fairfax of Roxburghshire. Charlecote, where they soon went to live, was hers by inheritance; her signature had to be put to all legal documents. Under a new and unsentimental stewardship not only pictures, china, furniture had to go but farms and land too, and Ada, who had been brought up to reverence and worship every stone of the place, every blade of grass, had to be the one to sign them away. When she found that neither refusals to sign, tears or sulks had any effect, and that no pathetic plea of hers would soften her husband's intention not to allow the estate to be burdened with any more dead wood, she signed. The sweet biddable girl turned into a fretful, complaining wife; the light foot, the tiny waist, vanished after ten pregnancies; her face set early into lines of middle age.

By taking on Charlecote, Henry Fairfax assumed a burden of whose weight he should have been warned, but he had a flair for estate management and had there not been a 1918 war he might, with severe retrenchment, have pulled it round, only to have it founder in the final landslide of the great estates. He had his own *amour propre*; when he appeared in the hunting field he felt himself being measured against the image of his wife's genial popular father, and found wanting. He was not himself a genial man and did not seek popularity. His mother-in-law he despised since she had not herself been able to provide a son; though he was not above working on her feeling for Charlecote to make her pay for *his* four sons' education.

Six children lived, wore out each other's clothes, fed rather worse than the cottagers' children. They avoided their parents, were comforted and fed by the head groom's wife and plotted for themselves a secret life out of sight of the windows of their father's business room, where he sat dictating endless letters to *The Times* and *Morning Post* on the plight of the landowner. He was not alone in doing this. All over the country others like himself were experiencing the shrivelling draught of change. A chilly fear had crept in during the closing years of the nineteenth century that the old way of life, so seemingly entrenched, so hallowed in history, was on the way out.

The sun came briefly out in Warwickshire when Edward VII came to the throne, and the County sunned itself in the King's frequent visits to Lady Warwick (whose wedding Mary Elizabeth had attended) at the castle and Lady Mordaunt at nearby Walton Hall. Many of the larger houses in the neighbourhood were rented by *nouveaux riches* and the small fry who swim in the wake of royalty. There were shooting parties and balls but the Lucys were not asked to them any more. Her husband's unpopularity extended to Ada, who, resenting patronage, snubbed even her old friends. She was bitterly resentful of those who could afford to keep up the old standards. In 1939 it was easier to give in and accept her husband's decision to leave Charlecote to caretakers and, for the duration of the war, live up in Scotland in his substantial stone villa on the banks of the Tweed, a lovelier river than the Avon, but this she would never admit. She died there in 1942.

By the end of the Second World War it was to be seen that Charlecote's long day as a family home was over. The farms were all sold with the Queen Anne parsonage house at Hampton Lucy and the greater part of the villages of Charlecote and

Hampton Lucy—so long in Lucy ownership. The benevolent Squire, with respectful cottagers curtseying at their doors and the fire-flushed cottage interiors so beloved of Victorian *genre* painters, had passed into legend.

I first saw Charlecote in the mid-1930s as a young girl engaged to be married to the second son of the house. The welcome I received was chilly.

Ada, my mother-in-law to be, had reduced the problem of upkeep by shrouding all but a few rooms in dust sheets. Blinds drawn down made a yellow daylight in these unvisited rooms. She believed, pathetically as I saw, that possessions thus protected would return to pristine use when the good days returned. For Ada, it must be remembered, came from a long line of landowners who had from time to time married money (and spent it royally); who had complained about income tax when Pitt was prime minister, about the folly of educating the lower classes, about the fall in farm rents in the bad agricultural years of the 1870s and '80s, and inveighed helplessly and ineffectually against rising taxation and death duties under Lloyd George. It is my belief that she thought that if Charlecote could be run on minimal household expenditure, to bridge this uncomfortable shivering interim, it could come to be lived in again, though perhaps not quite so fully as in her father's day.

In winter the cold was like a presence in the house. My father-in-law caused the wasteful, elegant grates to be removed from the bedrooms and replaced them with mean small ones that only burned two lumps of coal in, he said, the interest of economy, but in fact to prevent his wife's relations from coming to stay. He did not economise on hunters for himself. I brought with me reverberations from the outside world that jarred on them. I could fancy them saying, 'She can never understand us. Perhaps he won't marry her. They'll never live here.' Outpaced by the future, they died, and everything changed. For nearly thirty years I was virtually mistress of Charlecote under the wing of the National Trust.

Like so many before me, I came to love it dearly, but the girl I was had everything to learn about what the reconciling hand of Time can do to the relationship that grows between people and places. For a long time I found it hard to forgive what Mary Elizabeth and her husband did to Charlecote in their zeal for improvement, but discovering as I went along so much more about them, I was able to see inside their minds and perhaps had I been in their shoes I would not have done differently. Their comfortable certainty that anything the Elizabethans did they could do better excused the enlarging, the trimming up, the patching, the substitution of ancient crumbling brickwork for what was new and ugly. They did it with reverence and absolute belief in the future.

In the 1950s I became the chronicler of Charlecote and the Lucy family, conscious of my lack of qualifications as a historian. In the evenings, after the house was closed to visitors, I would carry my notes into the library to write there, but often during the day I worked in the upstairs room that had been Mary Elizabeth's boudoir; and it was there that I came on the five black notebooks in the drawer of her daven-port—a sort of Victorian writing-desk that you cannot get your knees under and which has a sloping top off which papers slide.

There was nothing remarkable in a Victorian lady with a houseful of servants and time on her hands settling down at her desk by the fire to write her recollections. What surprises us is that she was an old woman in her eighties when she began to do this, recalling the events of her long life as freshly as if it had all happened yesterday, as if in fact it was still happening, for each stage of her life that she describes is charged with the feelings of that moment—she feels it all again: the emotions of the child who fell out of the swing, the bride who fainted at the altar, the bereaved mother. Such total recall must be rare, and during my search through some 500 years of Lucy family papers, it was she alone who rose up, palpable, vivid and real—and with her the age in which she lived.

Now as the notebooks go back once again into the drawer they came out of, I look round the room that was her refuge in old age and think about how eager she was to please, how ready to love and be loved, how courageous she was. Whether looking at her portrait as the young mistress of Charlecote, with white shoulders displayed in ruby velvet cut low, or her photograph as an old woman wrapped in a shawl, there is in her expression ease and serenity, and I marvel at the protection afforded her through so many sorrows and afflictions by her conviction, which was one of the age in which she lived, that a merciful Providence had ordained it all for the best.

Chronology

1803 Mary Elizabeth Williams is born
1823 Mary Elizabeth marries George Lucy
1824 William Fulke is born
1826 Emily is born
1828 Caroline (Carry) is born
1830 Spencer is born
1834 Herbert Almeric is born
1836 Reginald Aymer is born
      Restoration at Charlecote completed
1838 Herbert Almeric dies
1839 Edmund Davenport is born
1840–1842 The Grand Tour
1840 Edmund Davenport dies
1842 Berkeley is born at Nancy
1845 George Lucy dies aged 56 (his wife is 42)
1847 Duchess of Sutherland's Ball
      Emily's wedding to Tom Fitzhugh
1848 Fulke dies. Spencer succeeds, aged 18
1849 Saxon church pulled down
1850 The burglary
      Carry's first 'drawing room'
1851 The Crystal Palace
      The Eisteddfod
      Mr Thomas appears on the scene

1853   The church at Charlecote is completed
1855   Reginald Aymer dies and is buried in the new mausoleum
1859   Carry and Pawlett Lane are married
1863   The Pawlett Lanes return from India
1864   Visit to Scotland
       Carry dies
1865   Spencer marries Tina Campbell
1866   Ada Lucy is born
1867   Linda Lucy is born
1870   Sybil Lucy is born
1871   Pawlett Lane remarries
1872   Fire at Warwick Castle
       Joyce Lucy is born
1874   Rev John Lucy dies aged 85
1875   Visit to Mrs Campbell in Scotland
1876   MEL and Emily visit Droitwich spa
1879   Shakespeare Memorial Theatre opens
1879   Mr Thomas marries
1881   Lord Brooke's wedding
1882   Flooding at Charlecote. Crops spoiled
1883   Ada comes out
       Lord Hertford dies
       Journals are brought up to date (MEL is 80)
1885   Spencer gives up his grouse moor for financial reasons
1888   Spencer begins to sell off his father's collection of paintings
1889   MEL dies
       Spencer dies six months later